Acton,
Carpe Diem!
DML

For Brett, my beautiful boy. Feel my love.

Maddie's Magic Markers

Maddie's Magic Markers Series

Purple Marker (Six)

Kill Like a Predator

ISBN 10: 0-9744097-5-8

ISBN 13: 978-0-9744097-5-7

Library of Congress Control Number: 2012910455

Published by David Mark Lopez

Bonita Springs, FL

Story and Illustrations by David Mark Lopez

Cover Design by Eileen Laibinis

Printed in the United States of America

All of the books in the Maddie's Magic Markers series were written, illustrated and published by their author, David Mark Lopez. Maddie's Magic Markers is intended to be a series of twelve historical adventures. If you have any comments or questions about the series, or have suggestions for Maddie's future travels please contact the author. He can be reached by phone at 239 405 3633, by mail at 3441 Twinberry Court, Bonita Springs, FL 34134 or by email at Jazzpop@aol.com. You may also purchase the books using a credit card through the website, www.davidmarklopez.com

DINO-WORLD

DAY 436 / ORION

I could see him, but I was pretty sure he hadn't seen me. Not yet anyway. But I knew that he could smell me. It's funny how they watch you with that whale-eye thing, where they can just stare at you from one side of their head without turning to look directly at you. He was so close I could smell the rancid guts barely dangling from his bloody teeth. I bet he'd enjoyed that disgusting two-week old snack I had laid out for him, but I knew what he was craving. He wanted exactly the same thing I did: some fresh, hot meat. Well, Big Al, we'll see who eats tonight.

His reptile-like eye was slowly circling around and his breathing was heavy and slow. I was desperately trying to bring my heart rate down and control my fear. Slow shallow breaths, no movement. If I didn't betray my position, he had to get closer and closer to find me. I let my mind drift for just a moment: the canyon, the river, the tree, the cave, the waterfall, the million near-death moments that had brought me to this time and place. A gust of wind moved the leaves around me ever so slightly.

Failure was not an option. There was no reset button. The Albertosaurus snapped his head back, greedily licking the last bit of rotting meat from his teeth. He slowly moved forward swaying from side to side. Three more steps. I tried not to think about my last two failed attempts or the hunger that was gnawing my stomach. The stinging gash on my left thigh reminded me of how one small mistake, one tiny miscalculation had nearly cost me my life. What was Dad always saying: Plan for the worst, hope for the best? My plan had better work this time.

It had been many weeks since I'd eaten any meat. I could survive on the plants and roots, but I'd had enough salad to last me a lifetime. I was no vegetarian. Two more steps and the hunt would be on. Carnivore versus carnivore. Predator versus predator. Man against beast. Me against YOU. He had the advantages of size and speed and power, but I had a much bigger brain, cunning, and opposable thumbs. Up your butt with a coconut, big fella. I could almost taste the grilled dinosaur filet melting in my mouth. The only thing missing would be the twice-baked potato.

Now he was inches away. If he could smell fear, I was already dead. I could see the tiny, lime green scales that surrounded his eye sockets and even the bloodshot veins in the corner of his large yellowish eye. The warm breath from his nostrils almost made me gag. Almost time: no blowtorch, no thermonuclear weapon, no machine gun. Just me, and Dad's Leatherman. I glanced down at the open, recently sharpened steel blade. I inhaled one last deep breath. I held the knife close to my chest in my left hand with the blade pointing outward. One...tick...two...tock...three...NOW!!!!

I ferociously swung the blade outward and downward as I simultaneously began to leap out of the tree toward the ground. I felt the blade connect and sink deeply into the giant prehistoric eye and felt it reach bone before I pulled it back. His head jerked instinctively toward me and he snapped the empty air I had just vacated. The Albertosaurus' horrifying scream filled the valley and I knew that every scavenger within five miles was now on red alert. I felt the hot dinosaur blood spurt onto my face as I barrel-rolled to the ground and came up running. "You got blood on your face, you big disgrace, waving your STEEL all over the place...we will, we will ROCK YOU!"

As I hit full stride I knew that the half-blinded monster was already in full revenge mode. I closed the blade against my leg as carefully as I could, and made certain it slipped into the dino-skin pouch around my waist. Without the knife this whole dangerous mission was a complete waste of time. I wanted to get ahead, but not too far ahead, so I glanced back to make sure that Cyclops was in full pursuit. The thunderous quake of his footsteps told me everything I needed to know. I deliberately ran the path I had traced so many times before (a deathly obstacle course which had taken me weeks to build) with plenty of cutbacks to slow down a twenty-eight foot, three-ton eating machine. I rock-hopped over the boulders where I had tripped and fallen a few weeks before.

I couldn't afford to look back again, but I knew from the pounding and grunting he wasn't far behind. The sweat was running down my face, and I had the taste of salty Albertosaurus' blood in my mouth. Tastes like chicken. So far everything was working perfectly. Just a little bit farther and I'd be home free.

I should have known the tree root was there. I should have known because I'd seen it a dozen times before. I should have known because when you are running for your life from a ferocious predator, you can't afford to make one single mistake. I should have seen it because when you fail to plan, you plan to fail. Right, Dad? I saw it a half second too late. My left foot got caught under the stupid root, and I went sprawling and flying in a jumbled heap of flailing arms and legs. I smacked my face on a rock so hard I cut my mouth, and I think I may have even broken a tooth. No time to worry about that. I looked up just in time to see the blinded, bloody beast go flying over the top of me. I'll never know how an animal that big got airborne, but that was definitely a flying ton of di-no-mite. Love to see those baby dinosaur arms flapping.

Crap and double crap. Now my plan was in the toilet. I scrambled to my feet and realized that I had almost made it. My heart sank. I was just a few feet away, but between me and my goal was a completely ginormous, slobbering, stinky, bloody prehistoric monster. I thought for just a second about how hungry I was, and that if I somehow got out of this mess it would take me weeks of really hard work to get all of this in place again. Then I noticed that Big Al was having a little trouble getting his bearings, and was struggling to get up. Maybe he had hit his head too? Whatever. It was time to act. I got up a head of steam and leaped from boulder to boulder and made one last jump onto the dazed dino, and finally up and over his razor-sharp snapping teeth of certain death. I closed my eyes and landed with a thud. Incredible...I made it!

NO TIME TO CELEBRATE...whatever problems Al was having, he was finally back on his feet and chasing me again in hot-blooded pursuit. But he was a day late and a dollar short. I hit the edge of the canyon at full speed with my arms pumping and my legs churning. I grabbed my vine swing in mid-flight, swung across like I'd practiced so many times and safely landed on the other side of the chasm. As I was trying to get my footing I turned and looked behind me just in time to see my evil nemesis skidding and screaming down, down, down over the rocks and onto the canyon floor. Ouch. That's gonna leave a mark.

I was really hoping the fall would kill him and make my job so much easier, but no such luck. He was bruised and bloody, but not defeated. His right eye was dangling by some strings and he was limping but he wasn't giving up. I knew that I had to finish him off quickly, because just about a month ago one of these guys, to my great surprise, had somehow miraculously managed to pick and scramble his way up and out of the canyon, ruining weeks of hard preparation.

He looked up at me and tilted his head and made a clicking sound with his throat. Did he know that he was trapped? Did he know that I was the one that had tricked him into his certain death in this blocked-off narrow canyon? If he did, he didn't let on. He threw his head back and let out a primordial scream that brought the fear right back up into my throat. Time to finish the job.

I didn't get any pleasure out of killing these magnificent animals, but I knew that if I wanted to survive, I had to eat. I also knew from hard won, first-hand experience that he wouldn't hesitate to eat me the nano-second he had the chance. This was the undeniable law of the Cretaceous jungle I found myself in: kill or be killed, eat or be eaten. He was never going to survive with only one eye anyway. The tyrant king I often heard roaring far down below the waterfalls would see to that.

I began pushing the heavy boulders (that I had painstakingly worked into place the week before) off the edges of the canyon. I hoped the job would be finished easily and quickly, and sure enough one of these large jagged slabs found its mark. I saw the Albertosaurus' crushed and bloody skull underneath the massive stone, and I watched the last twitches of life go out of his muscular body. Then I located my hidden pack, and scrambled down the rocky walls of the canyon.

Again I realized I needed to work quickly before the scavengers arrived to deprive me of my kill. There would be plenty left over for everyone to eat well tonight, but my needs came first. I fished my sticky knife out of my pouch and then used the Leatherman to quickly and efficiently carve out the best cuts of meat. It was easy once you got past the hide. Taking only enough to cure and smoke, I filled my pack and left the rest. If I didn't lose any to the bugs or the night thieves I wouldn't have to kill again for a few weeks. I would come back tomorrow and see if there was anything left to use as bait for my next trap. But now it was time to go, because Team Velociraptor would be along any minute now to claim the leftovers. I knew better than to mess with those jokers.

I stood tall on the shoulder of the carcass of the dead beast and looked up and around the golden canyon walls. I tilted my head back and let out a barbaric yelp and raised my dripping knife to the sky signaling to all and anything within the sound of my voice. I was no longer Brett Evan Lopez, the wimpy kid from Florida. I was, Orion, THE DINOSAUR HUNTER.

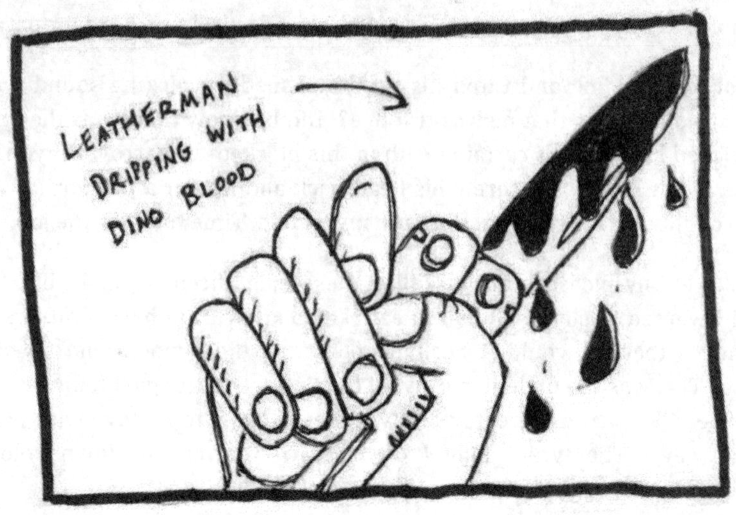

DAY 1 / BEFORE

Ok, I have a couple of confessions to make. First, I LOVE playing video games. So kill me. I would rather play video games than anything else in the world. In fact, if I could play video games all day long every day, that's exactly what I would do. I like playing them on my Xbox, my touch, my DS, my computer, my ipad, Dad's phone, Mom's phone, Maddie's phone, at home, in the arcade, in the car, on vacation, at school, with Joey, with Ben, with Jacob, with Austin, with Natalie (not my first choice), on-line with complete strangers, in a box, with a fox, in a house, with a mouse, here, there…ANYWHERE. Better than baseball, better than piano, better than reading, better than soccer, better than homework (definitely), better than ANYTHING.

Second, my Dad and I have a "complicated" relationship. Some people might even describe it as difficult. This isn't necessarily because Dad is crazy (which he obviously is), but primarily because of my earlier admission.

"Brett."

"Brett?"

"Brett. Hey, Brett?"

"What?"

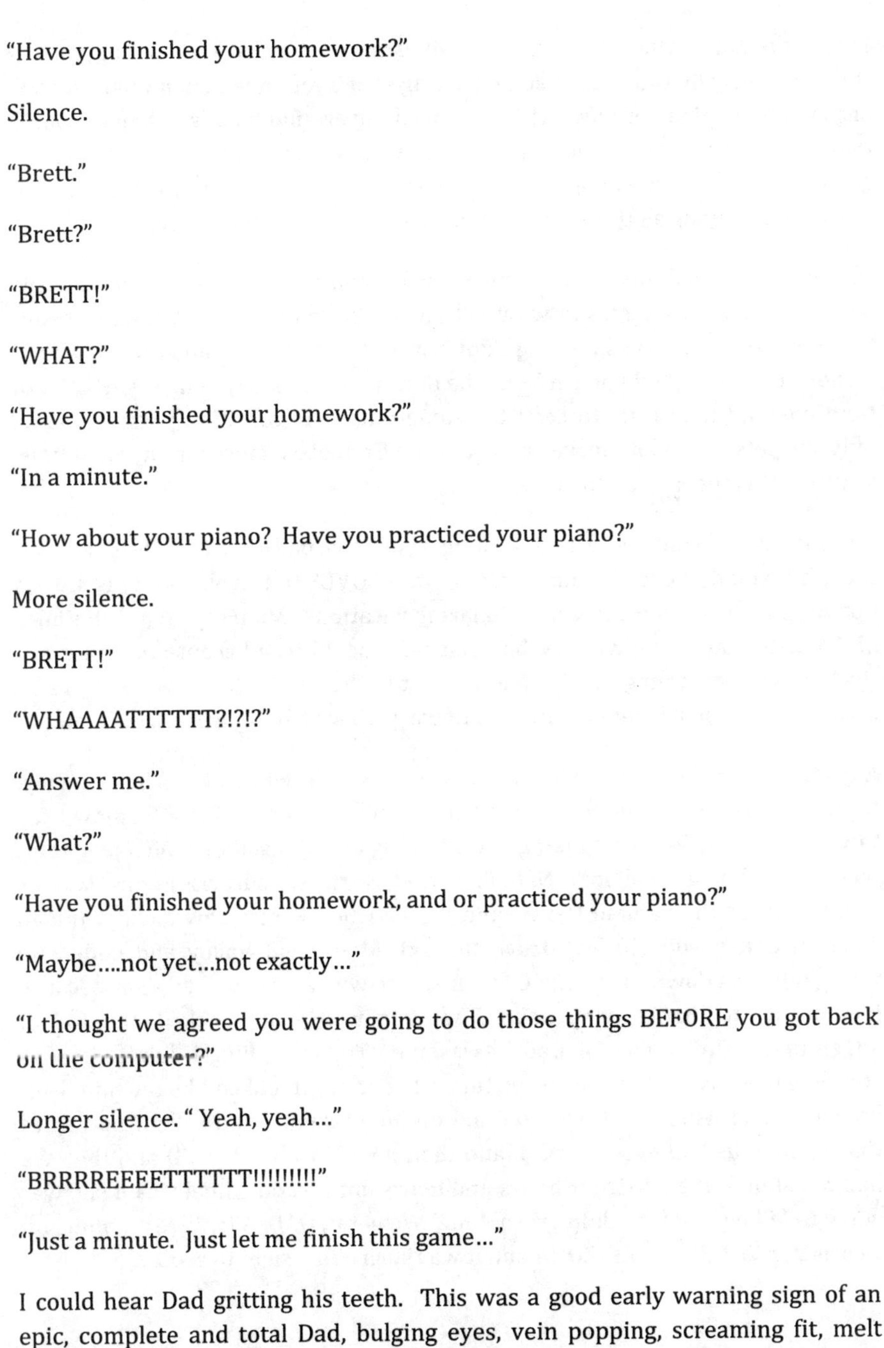

"Have you finished your homework?"

Silence.

"Brett."

"Brett?"

"BRETT!"

"WHAT?"

"Have you finished your homework?"

"In a minute."

"How about your piano? Have you practiced your piano?"

More silence.

"BRETT!"

"WHAAAATTTTTT?!?!?"

"Answer me."

"What?"

"Have you finished your homework, and or practiced your piano?"

"Maybe....not yet...not exactly..."

"I thought we agreed you were going to do those things BEFORE you got back on the computer?"

Longer silence. " Yeah, yeah..."

"BRRRREEEETTTTTT!!!!!!!!!"

"Just a minute. Just let me finish this game..."

I could hear Dad gritting his teeth. This was a good early warning sign of an epic, complete and total Dad, bulging eyes, vein popping, screaming fit, melt down.

"Ok, ok, I'm going. "

This is the point where it would be really smart for me to keep my big mouth shut, but I usually can't resist some parting shot about how much I hate school, or playing the piano or how UNFAIR everything around here is. Then of course Dad can't resist saying something about how much he is looking forward to me going to college, me having a kid just like me, or that my brain is turning to mush from playing all those stupid video games, or all of the above.

Dad and I have had this EXACT same conversation at least several times a week. So that's the primary reason we don't always get along so great. He's always trying to get me to do something I don't want to do. If he would only leave me alone everything would be perfect. The only good news is that he's gone a lot of the time, and then I get to have the same dumb conversation with my mom, only she gets mad a lot quicker and bans me from electronics for days at a time. Warning: Psycho lady on the loose!

But I have to admit there is one thing about my dad that I really like, even though I wouldn't ever let him know it. Dad LOVES to travel, and he is always taking us on awesome, incredible, amazing vacations. Mom says that is because he hates to stay home with us, but that can't be all true because he drags her (kicking and screaming), and us along most of the time. Mom always says he's not allowed to plan a new vacation until we get back from the one we are on.

Anyway, one time we went to Arizona for a whole week over Thanksgiving. None of us had ever been to Arizona before, and it was AWESOME. I know I say "awesome" a lot. We went hiking and climbing in Sedona, took a pink jeep tour, went on a hot air balloon (Natalie barfed, surprise, surprise), saw Meteor Crater, visited the Painted Desert and the Petrified Forest, saw ancient Indian ruins in Canyon de Chelley, drove through Monument Valley and ended up riding donkeys down the Grand Canyon where we had a snowball fight because it snowed on Thanksgiving day. That trip was action-packed and full of adventure. A plus plus for Dad! Awesome. The only thing I didn't like was stopping in Winslow to have our picture taken in what looked like the middle of nowhere, and where Dad went on and on about some band called the Eagles that none of us had ever heard of and then he had to buy the CD and then we had to listen to the music for hours and hours until Maddie finally said she was going to kill herself if he didn't turn it off. We get it, DAD. We were standing on a corner in WINSLOW, ARIZONA and it was such a fine sight to see...

FUN THINGS TO DO IN ARIZONA !!!

So, I was pretty darn excited when Dad said that just us two were going back to Arizona for my birthday and that we were going to have another incredible adventure.

"Yeah, like what?"

"We are going to hike from the rim to the river to the rim."

"Of what?"

"The Grand Canyon."

"Seriously?"

"Yup-yup."

"How long is that going to take? A whole week?"

"Only one day."

"No way."

"Way."

"Can I bring my video games?"

Sigh. "No."

Well, it didn't really register with me then, but later when I got to thinking about it, I remembered how deep the Grand Canyon looked, and some of the things I read about it. This wasn't going to be a walk in the park or a picnic at the beach. This was going to be a REAL ADVENTURE. Dad goes on adventures a couple of times a year with his buddies, but he always says I'm too much of a baby to go along, that I can't miss that much school, that I have to practice my piano. But this time I was actually going. Wow. Awesome. The only thing I had to agree to was that I would keep a journal on our trip. Another point of conflict with Dad was that he was always trying to get me to write, even though he knows I hate it. This was followed by a very long and mostly boring lecture from Dad about all the famous people throughout history who had kept journals, and how it was one of the oldest forms of communication and blah, blah, blah until I finally gave up. OK, just this once.

"Dad, I was just reading that a lot of people have died hiking in the Grand Canyon."

"Is that right?"

"All the time. We're not gonna die are we?"

"Hope not."

So a few months went by and my birthday came (got some really cool new video games and apps), and it was finally time to get on the plane and head to Arizona. I hugged Mom and sort of hugged Natalie (cooties) and then Nat whispered something really weird to me. She said: Be careful and whatever you do, STAY AWAY from the markers. What? Ok. Whatever. I had completely forgotten all about the crazy markers Maddie and Natalie were always jabbering about every time Maddie came to visit. More about that later.

So a few hours later we got off the plane in Phoenix, got in the rental car and drove a few hours to our hotel right outside the Grand Canyon. After we checked in, I asked Dad if we were going to start hiking the next day, but he said no, we had to do some scouting first.

After the traditional Team Adventure breakfast (bacon, eggs, toast, grits or hash browns, coffee for Dad, orange juice for me) we headed into the park and stopped at the Mather Point overlook just to check things out. Oh, boy. The Grand Canyon is HUMONGOUS. Here are a few fun facts I learned: it's 277 miles long and up to 28 miles wide, it's over a MILE deep and is over 17 million years old. And of course the raging Colorado River runs right through the middle of it.

We also read all the warning signs about the people who had died in the canyon, because they didn't plan so well. They either didn't have enough water or they didn't have a map and got lost or they fell off the edge because they got too close to the ledge. These weren't just doofy unprepared tourists. On the list was an Eagle Scout, a marathon runner, experienced hikers and lots and lots of regular people – just like me and good old Dad. I got a lump in my throat and was beginning to wonder if this was really such a hot idea.

We got back into our rental car and drove the winding roads to the ranger information station, where we received even more bad news. They wouldn't tell us which trails to take for our rim-river-rim hike, because it was too dangerous, and they were sick and tired of rescuing idiots like us who shouldn't be trying to do stupid things like that. Or something like that. The ranger recommended we go down one day, spend the night at the Phantom Ranch, and hike back up and out the next. Unfortunately you had to book your reservation at the ranch months in advance, so obviously that wasn't going to work. Usually, it's a lot of fun watching Pops get into heated arguments with complete strangers, but this time he didn't have much to say.

"What we need here, Sparky, is a really good map that shows us which trail to use."

"Or a helicopter, maybe."

"Sure."

I followed Dad around the gift shop and he ended up buying a laminated map we could carry in our pack with us, and a book that described all the major trails step-by-step. Hopefully they would tell us everything we needed. We walked over to the El Tovar hotel, hung out a little while, and then drove back out of the park for a detailed planning session over some pepperoni pizza and a couple of beers. Just kidding. ROOT BEERS, Mom. RELAX. I looked over the map and Dad checked out the book.

"What do you think, Champ... can we pull it off?"

"I don't know, but it looks like you can take this trail here down, cross the river, follow it along the river for about a mile, cross back over and then come back up this way."

"So we would take the South Khaibab Trail down to the Colorado, then follow the River Trail until it runs into the Bright Angel Trail, which we can follow back up to the rim, correct?"

"Sounds easy, but I bet it's not."

"So how many miles are we talking about here, Captain? Let's take a look at our trail book."

"South Khaibab 7.1 miles, River 1.3 and...Bright Angel 8.1..."

"That's almost 17 miles in one very long day. Think you can handle that, Biscuit?"

"Absolutely."

"Great. Why don't you take some notes in your journal, so we will have a record of our plans?"

I reluctantly fished the journal out of Dad's pack, and took down a few notes. Actually I seriously had my doubts about whether I could really do this, since the most I had hiked in one day before was six miles on the Oak Creek Canyon Trail in Sedona and that was flat. We finished our pizza in solemn silence.

"Now it's time to gear up. What do you thing we need to take with us, Chief?"

Just a word here about the five million nicknames Dad has for me. I'm not sure he actually knows my real name, since he almost never uses it unless he's mad. On a regular basis Dad refers to me as: Fluffy B, Chief, Son, Sonny, Champ, Sonny-boy, Roper, Captain, Brett Lee Evan, Lee, Leafer, Smeigal, Brettly-phite, Phite-o-mite, Muffin, Biscuit, Admiral, Junior, Weezer, Squinky, Acorn (don't ask), Dingles, Dipwad, Dinghy, Dipthong, Dingleberry, Baby Fart, Muffin Top, Ricky Bobby, Eggbert and a few more I can't remember. Just more of Dad's lame attempts at humor.

"How about food, water...and candy?"

So we had this really long discussion about survival, and all the questions we should answer before we hit the trail. Once we got going we would have to get by with the things we had carried with us. There wasn't going to be a 7-Eleven along the trail where we could pop in and pick up what we forgot.

How far? How long? How hot? How cold? How dry? How wet? How high? How deep? How dangerous? How much weight? How steep? How flat? There was a lot more to think about and plan for than just food, water and shelter. Dad just kept asking me question after question (I think Dad was a Nazi interrogator in a former life) until I thought about all the answers, and everything we absolutely needed to be prepared for the difficult challenges we would face. I was starting to wonder if this was going to be any fun at all.

We finally decided that we would put these things in Dad's Camelback: turkey sandwiches, apples, Snickers bars, gorp (peanuts, raisins and M&Ms), water (both in the camelback and two Nalgene bottles), duct tape for boot repairs, water proof jackets, whistle, Leatherman multi-tool knife, small first aid kit, sunscreen, bug spray, headlamps, map, trail book, lighter, zip-lock bag for our trash and toilet paper. No need for a tent or sleeping bags since we weren't camping, but that was plenty of stuff. We read that we could refill our water at a spigot along the River Trail, but that you couldn't drink the water out of the Colorado River without boiling it. I was finally starting to get excited until Dad reminded me that I was going to have to carry the pack some of the time. We loaded up and I tried it on. Man, that sucker was heavy with all that water and junk. I kept wondering if we really needed all that crap. Hopefully Dad would let me wear it on the way down and not on the way back up.

We went to bed early, because the plan was to start hiking before dawn. If we wanted to be most of the way back out of the canyon before the 100 degree afternoon temperatures sapped our energy, we needed to get down to the river before 10:00a. I had a hard time falling asleep because I was both nervous and excited. The fact that Dad was snoring like a rusty chainsaw didn't help either. I tried counting sheep, but all I could think about was all those people who hadn't survived the Grand Canyon. Had we planned for all the bad stuff that could happen to us? Were we ready? Dad was notorious for forgetting stuff (he lost me once at Epcot, but I'll have to tell you about that another time.)

It startled me when Dad started shaking me.

"Ok time to get going, Scout." Hey that was a new one.

I got dressed in a fog, still half asleep and stumbled out into the darkness to the car while Dad checked out of our hotel. We drove back into the park, and found a parking space in the completely empty parking lot. We grabbed our gear and hopped on the shuttle to the South Kaibab trailhead, but we had the bus almost to ourselves. Maybe only crazy people got up this early. Maybe only crazy people tried rim to river to rim at the Grand Canyon in one day. Der.

When we got to the trailhead the sun was just starting to light up the eastern sky and the twinkling stars were going out one by one. We strapped on our headlamps, and I looked down into the dark abyss of the canyon. If we weren't ready now we would never be.

"Ready to light this candle, Ranger?"

"Let's do it, Pops. Rock and roll. Baby in a microwave."

Down, down, down we descended into the canyon. The trail was wide and well-marked and as the sun started coming up, the sky became lighter and lighter. The colors of the canyon walls began to catch fire, and everything was glowing in the dawn's early light. Now I understood why we were here. Why we had come so far and why we were risking so much. I was finally on a GREAT ADVENTURE. Awesome.

We made good time and I was really starting to enjoy myself. We switched off our headlamps and put them back in the pack. Dad let me carry the camelback for a while and I was feeling so good, it actually felt light. We started passing hikers coming up from Phantom Ranch, and even a few people passed us going down. I wondered if they were doing rim-river-rim. Dad warned me that we needed to pace ourselves, so we would have plenty of juice to get back up Bright Angel. What was really cool was that as we descended further and further into the canyon I realized we were walking down through the ages. We were going backwards through the history of earth's geology. Every five minutes was another eon. I tried to imagine dinosaurs roaming these majestic valleys. While I was daydreaming I tripped over a rock and almost fell face first right into some of that history. I quickly remembered all the people who had gone down into the Grand Canyon, but hadn't come back out, and started concentrating on the hike. Some parts were really steep and dangerous. Your focus needs focus.

Before long, we could see the winding Colorado River down in the distance. I asked Dad what time it was, and I couldn't believe it when he said we had only been hiking for a couple of hours. We stopped and took a water break and ate one of our apples. Delicious. It was starting to warm up, so we took off our jackets and hiked in our shorts and t-shirts. This was turning out to be an awesome day. We started descending again and some smelly pack mules passed us going up. About another thirty minutes or so and we had reached the wide river. We crossed a suspension bridge, and Dad took some pictures of me on the bridge. It wasn't hard to imagine how over the years this powerful river had carved out this massive canyon. If rivers could talk I bet this one could tell an amazing story.

We reached the half-way point by a shady grove near the river, and ate our sandwiches. I couldn't remember tasting anything so good. Dad warned me that the hardest part of the day was ahead of us, so we were going to take at least a twenty-minute rest break.

"Hey, Dad. Ok if I go down to that shallow part of the river and cool off my feet?"

"Sure, but be careful, Sonny-boy. Stay really close to the bank. I'll fill up the water bottles, and be down there to join you in a few minutes. Oh yeah, take a few minutes and write in your journal. You'll be glad you did."

I was feeling so good I didn't even bother to argue. I picked my way down to the river, and pulled off my boots and sweaty socks. I slipped off the Camelback and laid it near the bank. The cool river felt great on my aching feet. I was feeling really pumped, and all my fears about surviving the hike drifted away. We had made great time and basically had about nine hours of daylight to climb back out of the canyon to the rim. This day was turning out to be awesome. "WE ARE THE CHAMPIONS, WE ARE THE CHAMPIONS...OF THE WORLD!!!!" I felt like I was the master of the Universe. Had to admit this was way better than any stupid video game. I put my boots back on, sat down on the bank, and rummaged through the pack to find my journal. There it was. I knew I put a pen in the pack somewhere, but I couldn't find it. I waited for Dad.

"Hey, Dad. I can't find the pen. Did you take it out of the pack?"

"Here just use this one, Hemingway."

"Huh?" I caught the pen he flipped to me in mid-air. It looked strangely familiar to me, but I couldn't quite place it. I sat back down on the bank with my feet dangling over the water and started writing. Purple ink, and more like a magic marker, but it would have to do. I was humming to myself as I was writing..."We are the champions my friends...we'll keep on fighting nah, nah, nah, nah na-na...No time for LOSERS!!!" Then I started to feel really weird and light-headed like the heat was getting to me. Not awesome. I noticed this really strange smell, and when I looked down the ink inside the pen was glowing like some kind of phosphorescent liquid..."WHAT THE...?" I stood up and turned to say something to Dad, and as I did things got even fuzzier. I must have slipped on one of the mossy river rocks just below the surface, and I realized I was losing my balance. I twisted and grabbed for the bank as I was falling, and somehow managed to snag the Camelback. My feet went completely out from under me, and I could feel myself being pulled down into the cold current. I looked up and saw my dad just shrugging his shoulders.

I'm a good swimmer, but I had no chance against the mighty, raging Colorado River. I rolled and tumbled over and over again, down, down into the roaring rapids. The best I could manage was to slip the Camelback over one arm, because I knew Dad would have a conniption fit if I lost it. I must have hit my head on a river rock, because everything faded to black.

My real adventure was about to begin.

DAY TWO / CHANGE IS NOT GOOD

When I came to, I gradually began to awaken and took stock of my situation. I was lying flat on my back on some not-so-soft rocks, and my clothes were still soaking wet. I had a very large, swollen lump on the side of my head, which I slowly and carefully inspected. Didn't feel any blood, so I was probably going to live. I slowly sat up, wiped the drops of water off my face and leaned back on my elbows. What the...? Not awesome.

Wherever I was, it wasn't anything like the Grand Canyon. The raging Colorado River had been replaced by what looked like a shallow creek. The same shallow creek that was now soaking my boots. I pulled my feet out of the water, and sat the rest of the way up. I was still a little groggy, so I wiped my eyes again, and took a few deep breaths. Inhale slowly. Exhale slowly. Ok, that's a little better.

The massive granite canyon walls weren't anywhere in sight. I didn't see the bridge, Dad, any other hikers or anything that even vaguely resembled the place where I had fallen into the river. Weird. Very weird.

"Hello..."

Nothing.

"HELLO!"

Not even a cricket.

I cupped my hands around my mouth. "HELLLLLLOOOOOOOOOOO!!!"

A giant insect buzzed by. And when I say "giant", I'm not kidding. I did a double-take. This wasp-like thingy was about a foot long. No kidding. More like a bird than a bug. Hmmmmm...didn't see that in the trail guide book. I turned slowly, looking around me. I was in a mostly dry creek bed with about a billion rocks. All around this wide expanse were humongous pine trees that looked more like California Redwoods than any other trees I had ever seen. Ok, so if this was California, I was hoping Disneyland was right around the corner. In the far distance I saw what was probably a mountain range, but it was a long, long way away.

I did a slow scan up the creek bed and spied a very pleasant surprise. Floating upside down, about 100 yards up, was the Camelback, gently bobbing up and down. Looked like one of the straps had caught on a snag. Yippee! This was like finding a long, lost friend. I stood up (a little too quickly – that bump on my head started pounding), and stumbled and ran over the rocks to my retrieve my pack. Astonishingly it was still in one piece.

I unzipped all the compartments, and happily discovered everything was still accounted for. No more sandwiches, since we ate those, but there were still some apples, the energy bars, the gorp and all of the supplies: headlamp, tape, whistle, bug spray (looked like that might come in handy) and all the other stuff. GREAT! At least I wasn't going to starve to death. Best of all, there she was: Dad's Leatherman! Usually he carries it on his belt, like he's Indiana Jones or something, but for some reason he left it in the pack. Since I'm not really allowed to play with knives (Mom won't even let me get a BB gun, for crying out loud), I was really excited about taking this baby out for a test drive. Later. First things first. Everything was soaking wet, so I moved to a little higher ground, and started laying all the stuff out on some flat rocks so it could dry. Ok, what next?

I noticed that the weather was sunny and it wasn't really cold or hot, but it was a little humid like a summer day in Florida. By the sun, I guessed it was about mid-morning, and I was getting a little hungry. I grabbed one of the apples and sat down. That's when I had my second surprise of the morning: about thirty yards away floating down the creek was Dad's adventure hat. Holy moly! I jumped up and raced over and grabbed it. It was mostly wet, but I put it on anyway.

Wow! If this hat could talk, it would have some awesome stories to tell. Dad's had it for about a million years, and has taken it all over the world. Very cool. But then I began to wonder what Dad's hat was doing here (not that I had a clue about where "here" was). Had he jumped in the river to save me? Was he around here somewhere? Was this some kind of crazy "survival" test he had cooked up? I was so completely and totally confused about what had happened to me, and what the heck was going on. Time for some hard thinking. I sat down on the rock again, and started munching on my apple. Well, Dad always says: the adventure doesn't really start until something goes wrong. Something was about to go horribly WRONG.

When the Ankylosaurus crashed through the trees about a half mile away I thought I was going to have a heart attack, and poop my pants at the same time. I was so startled I dropped my apple, and instinctively scrambled back a couple of feet. My jaw dropped open, and the half-chewed apple parts fell out of my mouth. HOLY MOTHER HUBBARD!!!! This wasn't just some lame-o animatronics from a theme park – this was a running, screaming, living, breathing dinosaur. DINOSAUR! Seriously, a DINOSAUR. You have got to be kidding me...

Before I could even begin to get my head around that mind-blowing fact, the roaring sound and the motion from the tree line forced me to turn and re-focus. OH MY G....I tried to speak, but the words just wouldn't come out. I couldn't scream, I couldn't talk, I couldn't even squeak. Now, I've been to a lot of cool museums all over the place, and I've seen dozens of movies and shows and videos, and I've stared face to face with SUE at the Field Museum in Chicago, so I knew exactly what I was looking at here. I was paralyzed with fear. Every muscle in my body constricted. My teeth hurt. My heart pumped in my ears.

The Tyrannosaurus rex bellowing and plowing through the tree line was easily the most glorious and amazing thing I had ever seen. His size and speed and power took my breath away. His roaring filled the air and dwarfed the noises coming from the Ankylosaurus. The thunder from his powerful legs caused the ground to shake beneath my feet even from this far away. I just stared at him in shocked amazement, too dumbfounded to move.

He broke into the clearing and quickly spotted his fleeing victim. Oh boy, this was going to be incredible. I unconsciously pulled my fists up to my face, and gritted my teeth. I wasn't sure if I could bear to watch this carnage. The ferocious monster caught up to his prey in three or four easy bounds. The terrified Ankylosaurus tried to turn and face his attacker, but T. rex flipped him with one swift swipe of his enormous tail. The heavily-armored Ankylosaurus rolled over and over, but somehow managed to regain his feet. Those thick plates on his back weren't even slowing down the Lizard King. I couldn't bear to watch. That all changed when I realized that somehow the Ankylosaurus was unbelievably back up on his feet, and they were both now charging STRAIGHT AT ME...!!!!

JUMPIN' JEHOSHAPHAT, BISCUITS AND GRAVY, FUNKY BUTT MUFFIN, HOLY FREAKING DINOSAURS....!!!!!!

It was past time to get out of here. I jumped up and started running like a crazy person. I didn't take anything with me, I didn't look where I was going, I just threw my head back and ran as fast and as far and as hard as I could. Dad's always making jokes about the dinosaurs getting loose on I-4 near Orlando at Dinosaur World, but this was no laughing matter. I was literally running for my life. I must have run about a mile, but when I finally hit the tree line I glanced back just in time to see the Ankylosaurus go down for the last time. He desperately whipped his spiked tail, but he missed badly. The Tyrannosaur's slashing, razor-sharp teeth ripped into the soft underbelly of the unlucky creature and it was all over in a matter of seconds. I crouched under a tree cowering in fear, but I couldn't keep from watching the T. rex feed. Just once he stopped devouring his bloody lunch, and slowly looked up. His gaping jaws were covered with blood and Ankylosaurus skin was dangling from his teeth. I could have sworn he looked straight at me, and my heart just about shot out of my chest. I stopped gawking, and dove into the thick undergrowth shaking with fear.

Now that I think about it and knowing what I know now, running was just about the dumbest thing I could have ever done. These near-sighted dimwits are just waiting for you to move. That's when they become the predator. The less you move, the more you cover your tracks, the less they know about you, the greater your chances of survival. But I didn't know that then. As I sat in the bush quivering and sniffling, all I could think about was what in the world I was doing here in...wherever...wherever I was. Was this the past, the present or the future? Wherever it was, it was an incredibly dangerous place to be.

I spent a long night in the woods. I found a dry spot in a thicket of some kind of plants and just tried to sit quietly and think. I'd like to tell you I got some sleep, but I didn't. Every little sound I heard made my fear return. Was the T. rex coming back? What else was out there in this strange world? Where was I? How did I get here? Was Dad here? I didn't have any answers.

I tried to calm myself down, by controlling my breathing. I wasn't doing myself any good by being this scared. Think logically. Then it hit me like a smack across the face. The markers! I was here because of the stupid markers. Dad had tossed me the purple marker, and just as soon as I started using it weird things started happening; the smell, the glow, the dizziness.

A little bit of history here. I first found out about the markers a couple of years ago. When I got back from the museum in Chicago, my sisters Natalie and Maddie were at our hotel going crazy, and asking me all kinds of stupid questions about some marker I had taken to make some drawings. I hadn't even been able to get the marker to work, so I just gave it to them and forgot all about it.

Then last year one time when Maddie came down for a visit, she and Natalie had gotten into this really big chick-fight over the markers. I was pretending not to listen, but I heard every word.

"Natalie, for the last time, you little middle-school monster, tell me where the markers are!"

"I'm not telling you. You threw them away, I found them and now they are MINE. Calm down, and go brush your hair or text your boyfriend or something. Brett, get out of my room."

"I don't care. You know they are dangerous, and if you-know-who finds them, then we are all going to be in a boat load of trouble. And I don't have a boyfriend. "

"Yeah, you are only saying that because you got to go on FOUR trips and I only got to go on one. Besides I haven't gotten them to work again anyway. Maybe you should try being nice for a change. Brett, PLEASE stop touching me."

"I am nice. See I'm being really nice right now. Feel my niceness. Just tell me where they are, and I'll get rid of them once and for all. Brett, please stop picking your nose."

"Not happening. I've hidden the markers in my top secret, extra special hiding place."

"If you can't get them to work, what's the point of keeping them?"

"I don't know. I'm still thinking about it. Maybe I want to go back and meet Queen Elizabeth. Brett, get your feet off my bed."

"That's the problem, Nat-ster. You don't get to tell the markers where you want to go. They just dump you in the middle of nowhere, and you have to figure it out. Brett, when is the last time you took a shower, stinky?!? Eww."

I don't remember exactly what they said after that, but I remember they just wouldn't shut up about it. Yawn. I got bored, and went to play Xbox. Awesome. I forgot all about the markers, but I have to admit a few weeks later I remembered them and decided to take a crack at it. It took me about two minutes to find Natalie's "secret" hiding spot (in the pantry behind the brownies). The markers were pretty cool, but five of them were completely dry. I couldn't get the caps off of any of the rest of them that still had ink in them, so I gave up. Every once in a while I would get them out and try it again, but I never had any luck. Worthless.

Now, it looks like Maddie was right. (Wow, I don't think I've ever said that before.) Here I was: alone, cold, hungry, scared and in the middle of some forgotten world where dangerous creatures who wanted to eat me lurked around every corner. It was going to take everything I had just to survive, and I didn't have many resources. In fact, I didn't have any resources. I have watched enough of those survival shows to know that I basically needed three things: food, water and shelter. Then I remembered the camelback. Some of the things I was going to need, I had luckily brought with me.

After the sun came up, I slowly and carefully picked my way back to the creek bed, taking cover wherever I could. There was no sign of Thunder Lizard, but who knew what was watching me from the trees? Eventually I got back to my pack, and happily discovered everything was exactly the way I had left it. Not to mention the fact that it was now dry. Then I looked down, and my heart sank. Right smack in the middle of a huge Ankylosaurus footprint was the lighter, busted into a million pieces. Crapola.

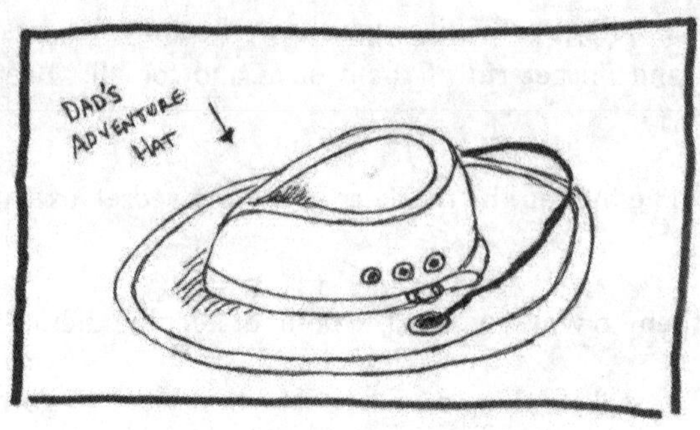

DAY 10 / TREE HOUSE

I have been living in my tree for about a week now. I started cutting notches in my belt to keep track of the time, but I may have missed a day or two in there somewhere. I also found the pen I'd lost. It was stuck down in the backpack wedged between the folds of the material. So, just to help pass the time and keep myself organized, I decided to keep this journal. The paper was a little water-logged, but it had eventually dried out enough to write on. Woohoo. Dad would be thrilled. So, this is my story and I'm sticking to it. My name is Brett, and I approve this message.

After I left the creek bed that second day, I started walking slowly and cautiously along the tree line. I really didn't know where I was going, but I thought it might be smart to head towards those mountains I'd seen in the distance. If I could get a little higher I might be able to get a better idea about the lay of the land, and find a good place to make a shelter. After seeing the T. rex, my biggest fear was that some gigantic dinosaur was going to burst out of the woods and eat me. I kept my eyes peeled and my ears open.

As the day went by I started to relax a little more. In fact the whole time I've been here the only dinosaurs I've seen are the ones I saw that very first day. Turns out that this world wasn't like the movies I'd seen or the books that I'd read where there were scads of dinosaurs all over the place, just waiting to attack you. Hopefully it was going to be like trying to see bears or mountain lions, where you had to be really quiet and look really hard. Dad always says that animals are more scared of you, than you are of them. If that were true, then it would greatly increase my chances of survival until I figured out what was going on.

"Hey, Dad? How come when we're hiking we NEVER see any wild animals or anything?"

"I don't know. Maybe it has something to do with the fact that you and your sisters make more noise than a herd of buffalo on steroids."

"Oh."

The landscape slowly but surely changed that day. As I kept walking, the gradual upward incline eventually turned into a series of gently rolling hills and the creek got deeper and wider. I finished off the water in my Camelback, and decided it would probably be ok to fill it up from the creek. I mean if I had gone back in time 100 MILLION years, the water had to be clean enough to drink, right? I tried to eat as little as possible, but I knew my food supply wasn't going to last very long. Maybe three or four days, if I was really careful. I tried not to think about it, but I knew that sooner or later I was going to have to start living off the land.

I've seen all those TV survival shows, so I had a half decent idea of what I was going to have to do. The only problem was that I hadn't seen any berries or fruits or nuts or rabbits or squirrels or anything really that would be even possible to eat. So, I guess I was going to have to figure out what the dinosaurs ate. They were gigantic, so they had to be eating something. Oh yeah: EACH OTHER. But I also knew that wasn't entirely true. I'd been crazy about dinosaurs since I was old enough to turn a page, so I knew that plenty of them were herbivores, not carnivores. Eventually I was going to have to figure out what they were eating. The thought of eating leaves and tree bark didn't sound too exciting though.

Another big problem was that I was burning a lot of energy with all this hiking up and down these hills. And I knew the climbing was going to get steeper as I got nearer to those mountains. Even though I had walked a long way, it didn't seem like I was really much closer. How long was it going to take me to get there? A week? A month? I didn't know, but I knew that I was going to run out of food long before I got there.

When the sun went down, I hunkered down for the night, and finished off the last of my Snickers bar. I found another dry area, and slept a little bit better. What would have really been nice though? A cozy, warm fire.

I eventually reached the tree where I am currently living. I ran completely out of food, and had absolutely no energy to hike any further. It rained for about three straight days and I had to fight my way up even steeper hills covered with slippery mud. I was wet and cold and hungry. Really hungry.

I found the tree by sheer, dumb luck. A couple of nights ago, it was raining so hard I couldn't even think about sleeping. The only thing that was keeping me even a little dry was Dad's hat. I was shivering and shaking and was about to curl up into a ball and die, when I remembered my head lamp. I dug it out of the top, zippered compartment of the pack and flipped it on. Still working. I slipped it on over the hat, and started looking around. After just a few minutes, I found a hollowed out tree. I pushed aside a couple of plants blocking the entrance and crawled inside. I was hoping it wasn't the home of some terrible tree-dinosaur that I'd never heard of, but it was basically empty. I chased out a couple of prehistoric, foot-long cockroaches, but they didn't put up much of a fight. Hey, I wonder how they taste? Anyway, I was safe and dry and finally got a good night's sleep for a change.

The next morning, I inspected the tree a little more thoroughly. Turned out to be really cool. Awesome. It was almost completely hollowed out, because there was another tree growing up inside it. Over the years the new tree had taken over the old tree and kind of strangled it I guess. I could climb all the way up the new tree by following the roots that had grown up inside the massive, rotted out base of the old tree. I started thinking that maybe this could be my home base. It wasn't far from fresh water, and would keep me warm and safe and dry. Especially if I could figure out how to start a fire, and get some of the dampness out of it. I could be like that dude in "My Side of the Mountain" or the people in the "Swiss Family Robinson." If I could just find a little food, I was golden.

I scraped out the inside of the tree a little more, and organized my stuff. Things were finally starting to look up a little. I climbed up in the tree as far as I could, and had a good look around.

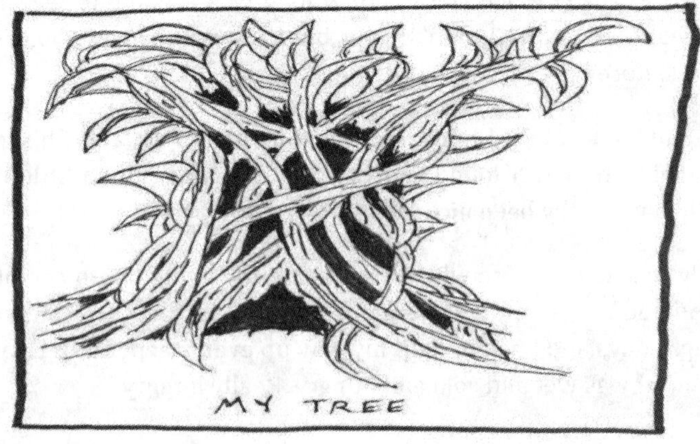
MY TREE

The bright, green canopy of trees extended about as far as I could see in one direction. In the other direction the mountain range gradually rose until it reached the sky. It was still a long way away, but I thought I could make out what looked like smoke coming out of the highest peak. Then I saw what looked like some birds circling and gliding in the mountain drafts. Pteranodons? These were the first animals I had seen in over a week (besides giant bugs and flying insects), but I was too far away to clearly identify them.

The snorting noises below me made me forget all about the flying animals in the distance. I quickly scrambled back down to the lower branches. I squatted down on one of the broadest branches, and quietly watched what was unfolding below me. I heard them before I saw them, but eventually three or four very large, mostly gray, long, slow moving dinosaurs came into view. At first I thought they might be Apatosaurs, but that would be the wrong era (ok, I'm a dinosaur nerd), and these beasts had three horns and armor. They made their way slowly through the thick forest underbrush, grazing on the broad leaves and giant pine cones. They were magnificent, and I watched them wind their way through the trees. One of them came within 100 yards or so of "my" tree, and I held my breath. I sat motionless and carefully observed them. I didn't think I was in any danger from these plant-eaters, but I certainly didn't want to find out.

From their horned heads I was pretty sure these were Triceratops, but it was really hard to tell through the thick branches. Occasionally one would reach its massive neck to the ground and uproot something near a tall, leafy plant. Eventually they meandered out of sight, but I heard them munching leaves and crunching the underbrush for several more minutes. When I was certain they were gone, I darted down the tree, and took a closer look at what they were eating. The first thing I noticed was a big pile of stinking poo one of these monstrous beasts had donated to my camp site. Disgusting. I was hoping I wouldn't have to inspect the dino-crap to figure out what they were eating.

Fortunately they had left plenty of evidence behind where they had been digging. Thank you. I bent down and carefully inspected the half-chewed roots. I knew a little about edible plants from my Boy Scout training, so I was eager to get a closer look. This was some kind of white, pulpy root from a plant I had seen plenty of times along the way on my hike. I sniffed it. Not much of a smell. I figured what the heck...if it was good enough for a dinosaur it was probably good enough for me. Well, the good news is that I didn't immediately throw-up, Natalie style. The bad news: it didn't have much flavor, but after I ate a few more bites I got used to the taste. I knew not to eat too much, so I waited to see if I could keep it down. I gathered a few more of the roots, and returned to the safety of my tree.

If the root was edible, then one of my major problems was solved. I also realized that if I sat patiently in my tree and quietly observed the world around me, I could learn a few things. Sooner or later more dinosaurs would pass through, and I could figure out what was safe to eat by watching them. I also got to thinking about my water source. Yeah there was plenty of it, but maybe there was something to eat in there also. It wouldn't be too hard to whittle a fish hook, and try to catch whatever might be lurking below the surface. The creek might also be a good way to observe some more dinosaur behavior. All mammals needed fresh water to drink.

Lots of ideas were swirling around in my brain, but I kept coming back to one thing over and over again. Whatever I found to eat would probably taste a lot better if I could cook it. I needed fire. Fire would keep me warmer. Fire would keep me dry. I could cook with fire. Animals were afraid of fire. Fire good.

So I determined that tomorrow I would come up with a plan to create fire. I knew it wouldn't be easy, but since I had finally found something to eat I had all the time in the world. I fell asleep that night wondering what a Triceratops burger would taste like...

DAY 56 / COME ON BABY, LIGHT MY FIRE

Life is good. No homework, no piano lessons, no sisters...no problemo. Most days I sleep as late as I want, climb up in my tree and just hang out. I like to climb as high as I possibly can and watch the changing shades of green on the canopy as the clouds pass by. When it rains, I stay in my tree where it is warm and safe and dry. I have found more than just a few things to eat by observing what the other mammals are eating. Occasionally I hear one of the monster carnivores roaring, but they always sound like they are a long way off. So far, so good. I don't see a dinosaur very often, and when I do it's usually just one of the slow-moving herbivores.

I've been getting lots of exercise swinging around in the trees, just like a lemur. Yo, Tarzan. I discovered that most of the trees have these long vines hanging down between the branches. I practice swinging around from tree to tree every day, and am actually getting pretty good at it. I had a couple of bad falls at first, but no broken bones as far as I could tell. Awesome.

My biggest problems are the bugs, which are evidently under the mistaken idea that my tree house is also their tree house. But they are mostly annoying and pretty easy to get rid of. I've even sampled a couple of the fat larvae I've found, but so far they've all tasted extremely disgusting.

The best news of all: I now have a fire, and have learned the hard way how to keep it going. I've even set out some traps, and am hoping to capture one of the smaller dinos that I see scavenging around from time to time. They look like Oviraptors, so maybe they have a nest around and I can snag some fresh eggs. My body is craving some protein, and I know that I have lost a bunch of weight since I have only been eating roots, leafy plants and a few figs.

Maybe you think getting a fire started is easy. It isn't. Nothing like all those shows and movies where they just whip out a couple of sticks and the next thing you know: poof, giant campfire. Now I have been in Scouts for a long time, so I have a general idea of how to get a fire going. But since I wasn't allowed, I had never actually started one all by myself. Sure I've helped Dad plenty of times, gathering tinder, kindling, smaller sticks, bigger sticks and then logs. But when we got it all set up, we always had something to actually start the fire with, like a lighter or matches. Since the lighter had been smashed to smithereens by Mr. Ankylosaurus, I was going to have to come up with my own way to make a spark.

Ok, the easiest way to start a fire according to the Scout Manual was steel wool and a 9-volt battery.

"Hey, Pops. Did you know that you could start a fire with a 9 volt battery and steel wool?"

"Right."

"Not kidding."

"What kind of terrorist training manual are you reading?"

"Boy Scouts of America."

"Now, I'm scared."

"Dad, where are you going in such a hurry?"

"To make sure we don't have any of those things."

No matches. No lighter. No steel wool. No 9-volt battery. There had to be plenty of other ways to start a fire, right? Right. Next...

How about a flint? I knew that flint was a certain kind of rock that could create a spark if you struck it hard enough. So I headed back to the river to see what kinds of rocks I could find. Just for the record even though I was getting pretty comfortable with things, whenever I left the safe zone of my tree I always kept a careful watch out for predators. I wore my Camelback and always had the Leatherman handy on my belt.

When I got to the water there were all kinds of rocks around, but I couldn't tell one from another. I tried a few different ones - striking them against one another and on some of the larger boulders, but I didn't see any sparks. I just kept trying different combinations over and over, but the only thing that got me was some sore and bloody knuckles. I must have been there a couple of hours trying to make a spark. No luck. I got so hot and sweaty; I took off my pack and took a break. I was so focused on trying to get a spark that I must have let my guard down.

I probably didn't notice the racket I was making banging the rocks against each other. But the Pteranodon that came swooping down surely must have. He gave himself away with a loud croak, and I turned just in time to see him gunning for my pack. Even though I was scared out of my wits, I instinctively dove for the pack and managed to grab it at the same exact second he did.

Filthy scavenger. He dragged me and the pack for about ten feet, but my extra weight must have thrown him off balance. He went skidding and sprawling and squawking over the rocks. When he scrambled to his scrawny feet, I still had the pack and he had a mouth full of rocks.

I wanted to laugh at him hopping around and flapping his massive leathery wings, but when he shrieked at me the only thing I could think of was to get moving. This was a giant animal, way bigger than any bird I had ever seen. And he was obviously hopping mad. Like I said, earlier I had seen them flying in the thermals above the mountains, but I had never seen one this far down in the valley and certainly never this close. I didn't want to wait and find out if he had any of his pals with him. I grabbed the pack, slipped it on and started running at the same time. I picked my way through the boulders, but it was hard to get up any speed. I looked back just in time to see him start running and jumping and flapping for a take-off in my direction.

I almost reached the tree line when he caught up to me. Not awesome. He lifted me up with the pack at the same time, and I could feel myself rising through the air. He had to make a sharp bank to avoid the trees. Just about the same time, I twisted around as far as I could and grabbed one of his talons that was tightly gripping the pack. For whatever reason, this must have frightened him and he loosened his grip enough that both the pack and I tumbled to the ground. He made a steep turn and started back toward me. I scrambled to my feet, and threw a couple of rocks at him. I don't think I hit him, but I was close enough to the trees that we both knew he wasn't going to catch me again. He flew off squawking and screaming, and I made my way back to the tree, bloody and bruised. Bleh.

So much for starting a fire with a rock. Fail. I tried it again later, but I didn't have any more luck. On to plan C.

My next big idea was trying to start a fire with friction. This basically involved rubbing two pieces of wood together fast enough until you get enough heat that smoke starts coming out. This seems to be the method of choice in movies and old Westerns. Since I'm not the most coordinated kid in the world, I didn't hold out much hope that this was going to work. But I didn't have anything to lose, so I decided to give it a shot.

First I gathered some old crunchy pine needles just in case by some miracle, I happened to get an ember going. Then I found the two driest sticks I could find which wasn't as easy as it sounds, since it had been raining on a regular basis. I knew that the only chance I would have was if my sticks were really dry. So, have you ever tried this? It's practically impossible. I had a hard time just holding onto the sticks tight enough to rub them together very hard. Then I started getting all sweaty and dropping the sticks. Then one of the sticks broke. I found a new stick. Then I started getting a blister. Then I threw the sticks on the ground and stomped on them. Then I said some bad words. Then I picked the sticks back up.

I had to find a way to hold one of the sticks still while I rubbed the other one against it. I spent another half an hour trying various methods of bracing "stick A" against something hard enough to hold it while I rubbed "stick B" against it. Whatever I tried: a rock, a tree, a fallen log, nothing was sturdy enough to keep the other stick from moving. I even tried twirling the stick in both hands with the point down into a hole in the bigger stick. Nada, zip, nothing. This was stupid. I was never going to be able to move the stick fast enough to generate enough friction to get a fire going. After both my hands were blistered and bleeding, I finally gave up.

After a couple of days of trying, I wasn't any closer to getting a fire started. Plus I had almost gotten myself killed. I waited a few days to let my injuries heal before I started thinking about it again. I really needed a fire. It would keep me warm. It would keep my dry. I could cook with it. And the most important thing of all: animals were afraid of fire. I was already getting sick and tired of being scared all the time. If I had fire, I could turn the tables and maybe do a little hunting myself.

My final big idea to start a fire was to use a magnifying glass. Now you already know that I didn't have a magnifying glass, but all I really needed was something that could focus the sunlight on one spot long enough to create enough heat to start a fire. It sure would be nice to have a pair of Dad's coke-bottle thick glasses with me. What else could magnify things? How about water? I had plenty of that but nothing to hold it in still enough to use it as a magnifier. Ice would probably work, but there wasn't any of that around either. Then I started thinking of all the things I had brought with me in the pack. Nothing came to mind that would help me.

I got out everything I still had, and spread it out under the tree. Duct tape? No help. Plastic trash bags? Nope. Bug spray? Forget it. Sunblock...

Then it hit me. My headlamp had a lens on it! I dug it out of my pack, and carefully looked it over. I didn't want to break it, because I knew it would come in handy. I had tried to use it sparingly to preserve the battery life. I managed to get the plastic lens part off without damaging the bulb. Excellent. I gathered some more tinder and kindling. I found the driest, sunniest spot that I could find. I put the tinder and a few small twigs on a flat rock, and took a deep breath. I held the plastic lens up flat above the pine needles and dried leaves. I was trying to hold my hand as steadily as possible to focus the sunlight on as small an area as possible.

An unexpected gust of wind blew everything off the rock. Are you kidding me? I patiently gathered everything again, and started the process over. Nothing. I was beginning to think I was going to have to climb the volcano and bring back some molten lava, when I saw the first tiny wisp of smoke curling up toward me. I'd never seen anything more beautiful in my life. A smile spread slowly across my across my face. Fire...you just got owned.

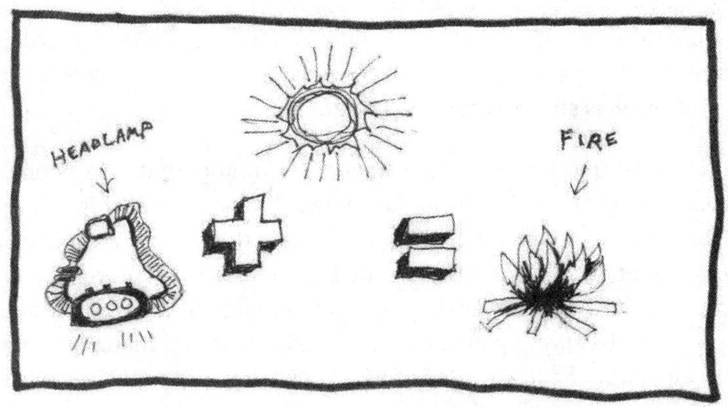

DAY 80 / BRETT'S VERY BAD DINOSAUR DAY

Thanks to the Raptors, my tree house has burned to the ground and the entire forest is on fire. I am now on the run. I am just taking a few minutes to write down what happened, because I have to catch my breath, and try to get just a little bit of sleep. I found a tiny little island way upstream in the middle of the river, but I have no idea if they can find me here or if the fire will jump the river and burn me to a crisp.

I told you that wherever I went and whatever I did, I was always, always, always very careful to avoid having contact with dinosaurs: big, medium or small. Like I said, I really didn't see one very often and when I did it was usually from the safety of my tree.

After I finally got my fire started, I learned through trial and error how to keep it going. I learned to always keep a few low-burning coals burning at my campsite. I figured out which wood was best for burning, and where to find plenty of firewood not far from my tree. I even was able to bring the fire inside the tree to keep me warm and dry. Admittedly this was a little tricky, but keep in mind this tree was huge; as big as the one I saw in California one time that was so gigantic they had a road going through the middle of it. No kidding. Like I said, I kept the fire really low, and I didn't have any problems. Until the idiot Raptors showed up and ruined all my plans.

With the fire, I was able to cook some of the roots and other things that I had been eating. It really didn't make it taste any better, but at least it was different and it felt good to have something warm in my belly. I knew that I was still losing weight, but maybe that wasn't so bad. I was getting really good at swinging on the vines. If I didn't slip, I could go for a long time from tree to tree without even touching the ground. Every now and then I luckily found a fig to eat, but mostly I was still craving some meat.

I was determined to catch one of the smaller Oviraptors that I occasionally saw pass through my campsite. They looked a little bit like a really big chicken, and I figured there was enough meat on those bulging thighs to make a pretty good meal. Unfortunately all my attempts ended up in failure. They were too fast for me to catch on foot. Whenever they got close enough to my tree if I made any movement at all they were gone in a flash. I tried tracking them, but they were so fast I really didn't have any idea of where they had gone. I was very wary of leaving the safety of my tree area.

I finally came up with the idea of setting some snares for them. I haven't ever been hunting before, so I really had no idea of what I was doing. I needed something the Oviraptor would step into and then when it tried to pull away, the snare would tighten around his leg. So I started gathering some large leaves that kind of looked like elephant ears and stripped off all the leaf area leaving nothing but the stem. I also stripped some heavier bark off the trees and used the Leatherman to poke some holes in both ends of the bark strips. Eventually I came up with something that had a chance of working. I had plenty of time on my hands, so I made about ten or twelve of them.

I set them up around the perimeter of my tree house in places where I had seen the Oviraptors nearby and where I had seen them feeding. I secured them to the base of nearby plants. I put some of my cooked roots in the middle of the snares and hoped for the best. A couple of days went by, and I finally caught my first victim. I was up pretty high in the tree, just hanging around when I heard the squawking. I quickly made my way down to the ground and was delighted to see an angry Oviraptor desperately trying to free itself from the snare. I grabbed a heavy stick of wood I had set aside to club my dinner to death. I made way too much noise, and by the time I got to my victim, he had seen me. I must have scared the holy crap out of him, because he lunged up at me snapping and scratching. One of his flailing claws scratched my face, he tore the snare loose and he was gone in a flash. I was in too much pain to follow him. Fortunately the cut wasn't too deep, and I knew I was going to live. I patched myself up with my first aid kit, and started thinking some more.

I was disappointed my snare didn't work. I had obviously underestimated the strength of my prey, so I went back to the drawing board. I found heavier, thicker leaves and stronger bark. I remade all the traps, which took forever. I put them back out in the same areas, baited them and waited. And waited. And waited.

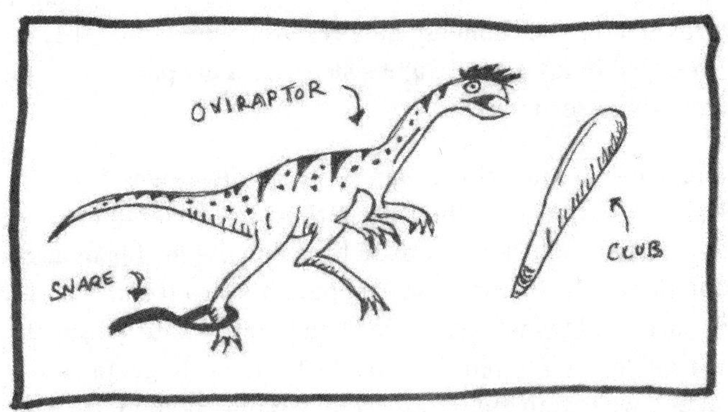

Finally I caught another one. This time I moved much more cautiously. I carefully and slowly approached the Oviraptor trying to avoid his direct line of sight. He was sniffing and picking at the snare when the club came smashing down on his head. I was pumped full of adrenaline, so I took him out in just a couple of strong, swift blows. It felt kinda weird killing an animal like that, but it didn't bother me too much. I was very excited about finally having something different to eat.

I dragged the dead Oviraptor back to my cave and used my knife to start removing the skin. Again, this was nothing I had ever done before, but I was determined to save as much meat as I could. After a couple of hours I had separated the dinosaur from his skin. I strung up the leathery hide on a nearby tree; because I figured when it dried I might be able to get some use out of it.

I went back into my tree, and blew on the coals in my fire ring to get them a little hotter. I added some more dry sticks, and in no time the fire was hot enough for me to cook my dinner. I put both of the dinosaur drum sticks on a long stick and started roasting them just like marshmallows. The grease started dripping and popping and the smell was incredible. I wasn't sure I was going to be able to wait long enough until they were fully cooked. I was squatting by the fire slowly turning the meat until it turned a golden brown. I couldn't take it anymore, and tore into my dinner. The meat was as tough and as stringy as anything I had ever eaten, but I think I can honestly say it was the best thing I had ever tasted. Awesome.

I wiped the dripping grease off my chin with the back of my hand. My days of eating roots, figs and leaves were OVER. I was starting to really enjoy my time here in Cretaceous World. If I could just avoid being eaten by one of the giant carnivores, I was going to be just fine. I cooked the rest of the meat, and hung it up to dry in the inside of the tree. I know what you are thinking, and you're right: this was one of the dumbest moves I've made so far. I let the fire die down and snuggled in for a good night's sleep with my pack as my pillow. I fell asleep in about three seconds.

I was having the most wonderful dream. My dog Buster was licking my face and tickling me with his whiskers. Buster is a Norfolk Terrier and we rescued him from our local shelter. Buster is mostly just too cute for his own good. Every morning Mom lets him my room, and he puts his two front paws on my chest and licks my face until I wake up. Since Mom knows I hate getting up and going to school, she finally figured out this was the best way to get me up and moving. I knew what she was up to, but I didn't really mind. If you had to get up, a dog alarm clock was probably the best way to go. Much better than one of Dad's eyeball-popping screaming fits.

The only problem was that Buster was starting to lick me a little too aggressively. In fact I wasn't enjoying it so much because now Buster was biting me. A little too hard. I slowly rolled over onto my stomach and opened one eye.

"Ouch, Buster...stop it...go lay down."

SHOCK AND AWE. I had never seen the kind of dinosaur before that was trying to eat me, but I didn't have any time to do a paleontological evaluation. He was half in the tree and half out and he was trying to rip my arm out of its socket. In my half blind state, I somehow recognized a piece of the stringy cooked meat from the Oviraptor hanging from his teeth. Stupid, stupid, stupid. I had no plan, I just reacted. The sweeping motion from my feet knocked him a little off balance and he turned loose of my arm twisting it more than a just a little. I screamed in pain and used my good elbow to smash him in the snout. Unfazed, he jumped back up to his feet and fully entered the tree. He obviously had been in this kind of fight before.

I rapidly crab-walked my way back into the inside wall of the tree, and tried to stand. He thrust his head toward me, and I somehow managed to roll away from his snapping teeth. I had no chance of escaping in the tight confines of the tree. I desperately needed to get out but he was blocking the entrance. I grabbed my club and took a couple of wild swings. He just stood there looking at me with his head half-cocked. Then I saw him put his head back and he made a trilling sound like I had never heard before. When I heard another muffled trill in response from somewhere outside the tree, my heart froze in sheer terror.

When the other dinosaur ducked into the tree and stood in the morning light streaming down from the rising sun, I stopped breathing, and the club dropped out of my shaking hands. Now I recognized them. These were Velociraptors. Hungry. Dangerous. Carnivorous. Time stood still. Two of them and only one of me. What were they waiting for – just get it over with. But they weren't looking at me...they were mesmerized by something else.

My eyes followed their eyes down to the ground, and then it hit me. They were seeing something they had never seen before. They were seeing something that got their attention. They were seeing something that frightened them. Fire. That was it!

By then my club was aflame, and I grabbed it out of the fire. The Raptors watched me and my fire-stick, greedily licking their lips. I thrust the burning brand at them, jabbing towards the first one and then the other. They took a step back, hopping and knocking the hot coals everywhere. I knew I couldn't hold them for long, so I decided to press my advantage. I swung the club wildly in a half-circle sweep trying to buy some time. I had to get out of this tree, before it caught on fire and burned to the ground with me in it.

With a flash of inspiration, I grabbed up my pack and started fumbling around while I held the raptors at bay with the burning club. I wanted to cry when I realized my fire was going out. These predators weren't going to be denied much longer. Flames started licking the inside of the tree, and the raptors inched toward me. I found what I was looking for, and madly pumped the nozzle on the bottle of bug spray aiming for their eyes. The roaring echo inside the tree told me I had hit my mark. They snapped and snarled, but they were missing badly. This gave me the few seconds I needed to start scrambling the familiar route up the inside of the tree.

Even though they were temporarily blinded they weren't giving up. The Raptors tried to follow me up the inside of the now burning tree. I could hear their claws scraping, and I could feel their hot breath when their snapping jaws got close. In a few seconds I would be out and free of these horrible monsters. I just kept climbing. I threw the whole bottle of bug spray down one of their gullets and that shut one of them up. How ya like me now?!?!

I had no time to waste when I got to the top. The Velociraptors weren't going to stay in that burning tree for long, so I knew it was time to relocate fast. I was trying to think of what to do next, when I was stopped dead in my tracks. On the broad limb about five feet away from me was yet another Raptor, and he was staring straight at me. ARE YOU KIDDING ME?!?! Tree climbing dinosaurs?

Never saw that one in any of my books. He leapt and I tried to avoid him, but his jaws found their mark.

AAAAAAAAAAAAAAUUUUUUUGGGGGGHHHHHHHHH!!!!!!!

I jerked away. I raised my arms and yelled, trying to distract him. Pain from my left arm flooded my body. The Raptor must have torn my arm out of socket. I could barely move it. Out of my peripheral vision, I saw more bad news. The other two Velociraptors had escaped the burning tree and were now stalking around on the ground below. Game over. No way was I getting out of this alive.

The tree climbing raptor idiot dinosaur had lost his sense of wonder about me. He crouched down, coiling for a killing blow. I looked up at my only hope. Just as he unleashed and sprang toward me, I jumped for the vine hanging down from above. As I was swinging I gave him a glancing blow which really must have surprised him. He teetered on the broad branch just a second, hopped back and forth trying to keep his balance and landed with a loud thud about forty feet below. I wanted to stick around and see if that killed "walnut-brain", but I didn't have any time to lose. I grabbed the vine, holding on with my good arm and hoped and prayed I could make it to the next tree.

It hurt like heck, but I made it. The Raptors below looked up at me in confusion, as the fire spread from my tree house to the surrounding grassy area. I hated them. I hated them with every square inch of my body. In a few minutes my beautiful, perfect tree house would be gone forever. They didn't care. They just kept following me from tree to tree, hoping I would make a fatal mistake.

The fire continued to spread and soon the whole forest would be on fire. The growing inferno distracted the Raptors enough that I finally lost them. I kept swinging from tree to tree until I finally ran out of energy. I dropped out of the last tree from a low hanging branch, and headed for what I hoped was the river. I had survived to live another day, but just barely. I had learned a valuable lesson though. Before I found a new place to live, I needed to think about everything that could possibly go wrong.

DAY 95 / ROBOTS, ALIENS, VAMPIRES AND ZOMBIES

You know how when you're playing a video game and the zombie/alien/robot/vampire gets you sooner or later and you "die"? You know how you don't really "die", you just hit that re-set button and start over? BOOM...instant new life! Well, that's what I needed, and somehow I got lucky and got a "do-over" in Cretaceous Pangea World or wherever the heck I had landed on my time-traveling journey of disaster.

After I finally ditched Team Raptor, I realized that camping out in the middle of the open forest wasn't really the brightest idea I ever had. Sooner or later in a position that vulnerable, I was going to be running for my life against beasts that were larger and faster than me. I decided my best bet was to try to head for higher ground where it would be harder for the really big animals to reach me, and where I could use my brains and my quickness to my advantage. Since I knew how to make a fire and how to get food, the most important decision now was finding a shelter that was easier to defend. Somehow, luckily I still had the Camelback and a few things with me.

The next huge issue was my dislocated shoulder. My limp arm was just hanging there like this really useless piece of meat. Whenever I tried to move it, pain shot up my arm like a sharp knife. I had seen enough sports on TV to know that I was going to have to somehow get my arm back into my shoulder joint or I was a goner. No way was I going to survive with all these predators around with only one arm. I cautiously tried pressing my shoulder into a massive boulder, but the pain was almost unbearable. I knew that I was going to have to do something drastic to get my shoulder back into its socket. VIEWER DISCRETION ADVISED.

I took about twenty paces back and started sprinting toward the boulder as fast as I could go. Right before I reached the rock I closed my eyes and turned my shoulder inward to take the brunt of the impact. OOOOOMMMMPHHHHH. I felt a really horrible pain, and then I didn't feel anything at all. I must have blacked out, because when I came to I was lying on the ground with the taste of blood and dirt in my mouth. I must have smacked my face on the way down because my lip was a bloody mess. Unfortunately, my shoulder and arm still weren't in place and the pain was worse than ever. Terrific. What I really needed was an x-ray machine and an orthopedic surgeon.

I backed up and gathered myself for another attempt. I put my head down and ran even harder. Run...jump...slam. I didn't black out this time, but the result was exactly the same. I lay there on the ground for a few minutes writhing in pain. This hurt worse than anything I had ever felt in my life. Worse than when I'm wrestling with Dad and he pins my arms back with his knees and thumps on my chest for about an hour. Way worse.

I dragged myself and my useless arm to my feet once again. Somehow I had to get more impact to force my shoulder back into its socket. I decided to give it one more try. But this time I was going to leap off one of the nearby rocks and turn my injured shoulder into the closest rock as I was falling to the ground. Maybe falling into the boulder would create more momentum than just running and jumping. I carefully picked my way up onto the highest spot I could find. Oh, wow. This was higher than I expected. Maybe this wasn't such a great idea. If I landed wrong I would probably break my ankle or kill myself. Oh well, my arm wasn't going to get any better sitting around and worrying about all the bad things that could happen. I carefully peered over the edge, judging just where I should land. I mentally went through how much I should turn my shoulder and the point of impact. I slowly backed up. It was now or never. I took a deep breath.

"One…two…three…GERONIMO…!!!!

It all went so fast, that I barely knew what happened. I slammed into the rock, even more pain exploded up my arm and the next thing I knew I was sitting on the ground, dazed but still alive. But there was good news: my shoulder was still hurting, but it felt like it was in the right place. I slowly rolled the joint around wincing in pain, but it seemed like it was going to be okay. What a relief. I figured that I needed to keep it in a sling for a while, so I cut some vines and wrapped it up as tight as I could stand. I still couldn't believe my crazy idea actually worked. I found my pack and started heading towards the mountains.

The good luck I found with my shoulder was only the beginning of a string of events where everything unbelievably went my way. If this was a video game I was easily advancing to the next level. As I got closer to the mountains the elevation changed and I found myself climbing up more than I was climbing down. I tried to stay as close as I could to the river I had found, since it was a little easier to make a path. The hardwood forest began to give way to thicker vegetation, and after a few days of hiking I was clearly in a jungle. Now, this was more like the dinosaur world I had imagined, and it reminded me a lot of the plants that grew in Florida.

I still was able to find the roots and figs that I knew were safe to eat, but I was starting to really crave some pizza. That little bit of meat that I had tasted, just made me hungry for more. I had plenty of water and enough to eat, but my belly was tight from not eating any meat. Every day my arm was feeling a little better and I eventually ditched the vine sling. My cuts and bruises from my scrape with the Raptors were almost healed. Every day I got a little closer to the mountains, and I was starting to relax a little. If I could find better shelter high up in those steep mountains then I knew that I could survive. There's no way the biggest of the dinosaurs could follow me up there.

After a couple more days of hiking and camping (no fires this time), I arrived at the magical place where I am writing these pages. Like I said the climbing had gotten steeper and steeper, so it was pretty much all vertical the last day or so as the mountains got closer and closer. This was some very tough climbing. As I came over the top of a ridge, I stopped for a minute to take off Dad's hat and wipe the sweat out of my eyes. I took a long drink out of the camelback, and slowly looked up. I couldn't believe what I saw. WOW...paradise.

Stretching out below me was a broad plateau as far as the eye could see. A series of three waterfalls came crashing down and ended in the middle of perfect lagoon, as beautiful as a postcard. On one side the steel, grey, towering granite mountain walls reminded me of Yosemite. In the other direction a lush green valley went on and on and on gently descending into a thick forest. To my amazement I saw herds of what had to be Diplodocus gently grazing on gigantic, leafy ferns. My jaw dropped when I saw a monstrous Brachiosaurus stretch his long neck to reach some leaves in the some very tall trees. There were literally dozens of Pteranodons swooping and flying up and around the thermals coming off the waterfalls. It was as beautiful as anything I had ever seen. Awesome. I instantly knew this was going to be my new home.

After I watched in amazement for about an hour, I descended into the valley and made my way towards the waterfalls and the lagoon. I knew this valley probably had its share of predators, but if these dinosaurs felt safe then I did too. When I finally reached the waterfall, I took off my pack, found a nice place to sit and got out my journal. For the first time since I had started my adventure, I felt like everything was going to be all right. No, not just all right. Everything was going to be GREAT. I wasn't just beating the robots, aliens, vampires and monsters. I was killing them.

DAY 132 / HOME IN THE VALLEY

It's all good in the valley. Well, it's mostly all good.

After I took my break by the waterfall, I realized that even though this place looked like paradise, it was no time to let my guard down. My original idea of living high enough to keep the big predators away was a good one. I still needed to find a new home that discouraged the carnivores out there from thinking of me as their dinner. Plus, I had no way of knowing what other unknown dangers were hidden behind, underneath and above this beautiful scenery. Up to now every single time I thought I had things figured out, there was some horrible disaster just waiting to take me out.

I cautiously started scouting around looking for something suitable and safe to call home. I couldn't build a fort strong enough, and I already knew that the hollow tree idea stunk to high heaven. Hmmm? What I really needed was a cave. A cave would be easier to defend and would keep me dry and warm. It had to be high enough to keep away the big predators like T. rex (no sign of this joker so far), Raptors and probably Iguanadons and Albertosauruses – even though I hadn't seen any of these bad boys. Yet.

I started looking up at the cliffs and the waterfalls. Way, way up I could see what was probably Pteranodon nests all along the sheer granite cliffs. No chance to get way up there. The waterfalls might be a better bet. Like I said there was a series of three waterfalls gradually descending down the mountain, each one bigger than the one above it. The constant roar from the bottom one was almost deafening, and the spray created a mist that was like a cool shower. This was actually pretty awesome, since the weather here in this jungle valley was more humid and it was hot most of the time. So, if I could find a cave near the waterfall not only would I have a fresh water supply, I'd also be able to have a nice cool shower anytime I needed it.

"Hey, Pops."

"Wassup, Squinky?"

"The sky, sun, moon and stars. So when did you get back from your extended vacation?"

"A couple of weeks ago."

"Seriously? I hadn't noticed. Where'd you go after you dropped us off at the airport?"

"New York City, Cooperstown and Niagara Falls."

"Fun stuff?"

"Niagara Falls was incredible. You can walk down to the Cave of the Winds and stand right next to the falls. Pretty amazing. Of course you get soaked, so they give you a spiffy poncho."

"So why you are still wearing it now?"

"Because it makes me look incredibly cool."

"And awesome."

"Word."

"Tight."

It's really hard to have a serious conversation with my Dad about anything but when I remembered this strange talk, it got me to thinking. Water causes erosion, and these falls have obviously been roaring down the mountainside for a long, long time. Maybe there was a cave near or even behind them. Wouldn't that be sweet?

I picked my way around the boulders and got as close to the falls as I could. The constant, pounding roar of the water crashing into the lagoon and the house-size boulders strewn all around was scary and amazing at the same time. Everything I stepped on was wet and slippery from all the moisture and the moss. I thought about diving into the lagoon and swimming under the waterfall to see what was behind it, but the current was far too strong. I am a good swimmer, but no way could I fight my way through that powerful force. This was no good. Time to see if I could climb up to the second waterfall.

This turned out to be easier than I expected, because it almost looked like a path had been made by something up to the second waterfall. You couldn't exactly walk up it, but by jumping over a few medium size rocks and with a little hand scrambling, I made it to the top in just a couple of minutes. There was a narrow two-foot ledge that led around to the falls. Easy-peasy, boss.

Now this looked a little more promising. This waterfall was a somewhat more manageable, and not nearly as intimidating. It was less powerful than the one below, because the height it fell from was a lot less. I took off my pack and boots and waded into the churning pool. Hopefully this water was moving too fast for any dangerous critters to be swimming around in it. It felt great. Suddenly, I realized that I hadn't had a shower, bath or brushed my teeth the entire time I had been on this trip. Two enthusiastic thumbs up!

The water got deeper, and I was eventually swimming in the swirling water and mist. I kicked my way under the main force of the water, and came up on the other side of the pounding surf. It was a little darker, but I could still mostly make out what was in front of me. I couldn't believe my eyes as I waded up and out of the water. There it was – a cave just like the one I had imagined. YES! It had a broad ledge, and I was pleasantly surprised that I could get to the cave without even having to go through the waterfall. This was going to be perfect. Time for the double-fist pump. Ouch. Forgot about my sore shoulder.

It took me several days to clear out the cave and claim it for my own. Several of the bugs living there took exception to me starting a fire in their "house". After facing ferocious dinosaurs, I wasn't going to let a few foot-long insects get the best of me. After I got my fire restarted, I found some tar and figured out how to make a torch that would last for about ten minutes or so before it burned out. The bugs didn't like getting burned alive too much, so they finally moved on. I experimented with roasting and eating a few of them, but only the big, white grubs weren't totally disgusting. They were a little chewy, but actually not that bad. Don't eat the gray or green ones though. Bleh.

I also found some beehives not too far from the cave, and managed after several attempts, and lots of bee stings, to get some honey. Turns out bees aren't too fond of fire and smoke either. Who knew? So now my diet was expanding to include honey, grubs, greens and roots. Not exactly Burger King, but better than the same old thing every day.

After I got my camp in order at the cave, I begin taking reconnaissance missions around the valley. Since I had solved my basic problems of water, food and shelter it was time to find out what else I could use. I discovered that I could climb pretty far up the granite walls through a series of ledges and handholds. If fact, it looked like if I wanted to I could make it all the way up to the Pteranodon nests I had seen on my first day in the valley. Cool.

The higher I climbed the further I could see down the valley. Every now and then one of those massive predators would come crashing through the trees and giant ferns, chasing some poor helpless creature. The victims included Stegosaurus, Diplodocus, and a few others I couldn't identify. I was just glad they weren't chasing me. Even old T. rex made an appearance occasionally. He wasn't as fast as some of the other carnivores and you could hear him snorting and stomping long before you could see him, so he wasn't really a threat to me. You could literally feel the ground shaking on the valley floor when he got close. In fact, if there was any threat at all from the bigger dinosaurs, I just headed up to my cave. No way were they going to bother with all the effort it would take to get up there, when there was plenty of meat in the valley.

I was more worried about the smaller predators like the Raptors and Deinonychus. If they found me I was going to have to defend myself and my cave. I made certain I kept plenty of sharp sticks around, and I always carried my Leatherman with me. I was really careful with my fire and kept it low most of the time. Since I didn't have any meat to cook, it probably didn't even register with any of the carnivores. The herbivores were just busy eating leaves and bushes and trying not to get eaten themselves. The smoke seemed to get mixed in with the spray from the waterfall. Hopefully that was enough keep any predators out of my cave.

I started thinking about hunting again, and as time went by I set up my network of vines and put out some snares. I didn't have any luck, so I needed a new plan. Would a bow and arrow work? Even if I could make one, most of the dino-skins were too thick for an arrowhead to penetrate. What I needed was a way to trap one of these monsters, so that I would have the advantage. I was sick of playing defense. It was time to go on offense. Game on.

DAY 161 / NOT IT

Like I told you before, things had finally stabilized and I felt like I was finally in control of my situation. I had a safe place to sleep, plenty of food and lots of fresh water. For the first time in a very long while, I started thinking again about the markers, my family back in Florida and if I was ever going to get home again. Obviously Maddie and Natalie had made it back home from their historical adventures, but they never said how they did it. If they did, I missed it. I had no idea of even how to begin getting back home. The best part? I didn't really miss much of anything. My cave home was just about perfect.

I caught a glimpse of my reflection one day in the water. Man, did I look scruffy. My hair was getting pretty long, and I had probably lost at least ten pounds. My clothes were starting to wear thin, so I knew that I would have to figure out how to make something soon. Or I could just run around naked. I'm sure the dinosaurs wouldn't care. Woohoo! Jungle Boy on the loose.

As I grew more accustomed to my surroundings, I began to take longer scouting missions up and down the valley. My vine highway kept me high and safe from most of the aggressive dinosaurs and whenever I saw one, I just tried to stay quiet and let it pass. Those big boys weren't too good at disguising their approach. You could hear those monsters from about a mile away. The ones I kept a lookout for mostly were the Velociraptors. I knew they were fast and sneaky and seemed to have some kind of pack-hunting intelligence. I didn't want to mix it up with them again, since my shoulder was still a little sore from my last encounter.

I also started learning how to climb up pretty high on the cliffs behind my cave. There were just enough ledges and hand-holds that I could reach the massive Pteranodon nests high above me. Every once in a while I would sneak an egg away while they were out flying around. Wow, did that ever taste fantastic! I heated it up on a rock in my cave and it had to be the biggest omelet in the world. I would also try to find where the Oviraptors hid their nests, but that was a little trickier. They typically stayed near their nests, and they had a nasty bite. I did manage to catch a few of those varmints with my snares, but like I told you before the meat was nothing but stringy sinew that you had to chew forever.

So my days were filled with swinging around the jungle, scavenging for whatever food I could find and going further and further from my cave. Off in the distance I could see the volcano spewing ash into the sky and occasionally I would feel the rumble of the tremors. I didn't have anything to worry about though. I knew I'd get plenty of notice if the mountain blew its top. I also knew that volcanos could spit and smoke for years before anything really exciting happened.

I built myself a hammock in the cave and got things organized just the way I liked it. Every now and then one of the smaller dinos like an Oviraptor or a Troodon got bold and somehow would hop and claw his way up the narrow path to the cave entrance behind the waterfall. They would just sit there for a minute and cock their head looking at me. Like they were studying me or something. They were too quick for me to catch, but one swift kick sent them squawking down into the waterfall. A B C D...I will kill your family.

Once when I was climbing really high along the cliffs I noticed something very strange. A long way away, far, far down in the valley I thought I saw something that looked a lot like smoke. I squinted and rubbed my eyes, but I couldn't really tell if it was smoke or just the usual mists rising up in the humidity like it did most afternoons when it got hot right before it rained. Too bad I didn't have any binoculars. I definitely needed to know if the valley was about to go up in flames. I kept squinting and trying to focus, but it never got any clearer. Oh well. I reminded myself to check it out again the next time I was up this high.

What I did see for sure though was what I had been looking for. Far down on the right, nearly hugging the sheer canyon wall was what I hoped was a little, narrow canyon. If that was what I was seeing then I had finally hit the jackpot. That was exactly what I needed to put my big dinosaur hunting plan into action. I carefully picked my way back down to the cave, grabbed some supplies and headed in the direction I thought would get me there the fastest.

This was an area of the valley I hadn't explored before, so I didn't bother trying to find any vines. I was kind of excited, so I made good time. I probably wasn't as careful as I usually was because I wanted to get to the canyon and back before nightfall. I was pretty much running and skipping. Hopefully nothing was following me, because I was making way too much noise.

When I finally noticed the dinosaurs, I was completely surrounded. There must have been about seven or eight of them and they were all looking at me. I slowly reached down for my Leatherman, but I almost fainted when I realized I had left it behind in the cave. Stupid. Stupid. Stupid. No knife, no club, no nothing. Just me and these little bird-like dinosaurs who seem to be fascinated with me. Herbivores or carnivores? Hungry or full? Friendly or vicious? I wasn't about to stick around to find out.

I made a jumping motion towards one of them screaming and waving my arms and hands. Rule #1 of Animal Behavior? Make them think you are coming after them. They all flexed back a little and I seized my chance. I started running as fast as I could toward what I thought was that canyon I was looking for. And I hoped it was close...!!!

The tiny dinos made a quick recovery, and decided that I was more frightened of them than they were of me. Even though I was pumping my arms and running as fast as I could, they were right on my tail. Every so often one would jump up and nip me on the back of my legs or my arm. Ouch! I was ripping through some pretty thick jungle, but it didn't seem to bother them. They probably could go on like this forever until I just keeled over from exhaustion. Then they could gnaw my face off.

I tried cutbacks, switchbacks, zig-zags and every other maneuver I could think of. Nothing was shaking these lightning quick dinos. Then it hit me. These dinosaurs were just toying with me. They were so much faster than me, they could have ended it at any moment. So why weren't they? I finally had to stop and take a breather in the middle of a clearing. I bent over gasping for breath. When I stopped, they stopped. They just cocked their heads and looked at me. All of them had that same dim look. Like they were just waiting. Waiting for what? Then one of them reached his long neck out and gave me a sharp peck on the arm. What the ...? Then another peck.

I started running again and so did they. When I stopped, they stopped. When I ran, they ran. When I trotted, they trotted. I finally got so exhausted I just fell to the ground. They pecked at me a couple of times and tried to get me up, but I was too tired to move. Finally they all just wandered off clicking and clucking. My first game of dino "tag" was finally over.

I just threw my head back and laughed. Partly out of relief, but mostly because it was funny. I was surprised to hear the sound of my own laughter. It had been such a long time since I had laughed. The stress flowed out of my body, and I got up, dusted myself off and headed toward what I hoped was still the direction of the canyon.

Another ten minutes and I was there. It was even better than I dreamed of. It was completely closed in on one end and narrow enough for me to block the other end. I began working on my plan until it started getting dark, and then I headed back to my cave in the twilight. I couldn't help singing a little on the way.

DAY 200/ TRAIL MIX

It took me over six long months to get the "Canyon of Death" ready for my big experiment. Every day I got up around sunrise and hiked to the canyon. I eventually found some shortcuts and it didn't take me nearly as long as it did that first day. I knew that for my plan to be successful, I had to make certain everything worked perfectly. So, that meant just like with our hiking trip through the Grand Canyon, I needed a plan. I began sketching my ideas in the back of this journal and eventually I came up with something that I hoped would work.

The hardest part was filling in and blocking the open end of the canyon with enough debris that it would hold a monstrous dinosaur, the kind that I was hoping to trap and kill. Long hot days and hard, hard work. First the boulders, then the trees, then smaller boulders. Everything had to be dragged or pulled over to the canyon edge and pushed down into the canyon. When that massive job was finally finished, I had to think hard about how I was going to get a T. rex or an Albertosaurus or even a Velociraptor to follow me fast enough to fall into the canyon. I just kept thinking about animal behavior and how everything in their make-up was determined by instinct. From everything I had seen, when they were on the hunt they didn't stop and think about what they were doing. These animals weren't "Evil Incarnate" like they were always portrayed in the movies and on television and in video games. They just kept after their victim until they caught and killed their prey or until it escaped. But that didn't happen very often.

So, if I could get them to just blindly chase me down a pre-determined path, they wouldn't have a chance to put the brakes on. They would end up in the bottom of the canyon. Trapped with no way to get out. That would turn the tables and make me the predator and them the prey. It sounded easy, but I knew that it would be incredibly difficult. I had seen these monsters in action many, many times and I knew they moved very fast in short distances. What they couldn't do, because of their bulk was change directions so easily. I had to find a way to make them keep changing directions, but have enough speed at the end to go flying down into the canyon. Hopefully the fall would break their necks and I wouldn't have to finish them off. I was doubtful that would happen though because the canyon was steep, but not really that deep.

I worked meticulously on my plan and the path of destruction. Keep in mind I always had one eye out for dinosaurs, while I was crafting my idea. Gradually things started to come together. I even managed to accidentally trap one of the "tag" dinosaurs who had chased me earlier. I guess he was just running along and fell into the canyon. I heard him squawking and rustling around and gently peeked over the edge. I was deeply disappointed when he picked and hopped his way out of the end of the canyon I had tried to close in. Fail. After I finished the path I was going to have to reinforce that area. It wasn't going to do any good to do all this hard work and take the risk of being killed, if I couldn't keep my prey trapped long enough to finish them off.

I had a little bit of luck when I discovered several vines hanging down from some tall trees near the canyon edge. If I hit one of these going full speed, it was easy to see how they could carry me over to the other side of the canyon. I took a big chance and tested out my theory. I had gotten pretty good at swinging on the vines, so it worked perfectly. Awesome.

The trail was finally completed to my satisfaction. I practiced it at least four or five times a day, making certain I hadn't missed anything or left out any important details. One simple, stupid mistake would cost me my life. I mentally went through every possible scenario that I might confront when my victim was chasing me. I also spent quite a bit of time watching how the carnivores pursued and finished off their prey. Far up, high atop my perch along the cliffs I had an awesome view of the occasional murder that took place in the valley.

The next thing I had to consider was how I was going to kill my victim once I got it trapped in the valley. I had my Leatherman, but no way was that blade going to take down a massive beast that weighed more than two tons. I just couldn't go one-on-one with these bad mamma jammas. They would rip me to shreds, and stomp my guts out before I had a chance to blink. Eventually these animals would starve to death or die of thirst, but even that seemed cruel to me. I had to finish them off cleanly and quickly. A bow and arrow, a slingshot or spear probably wasn't going to get the job done either.

Then it hit me. These giant boulders that practically surrounded the canyon rim were the answer. If I could leverage them and get it just right, these massive rocks could smash the skull of even the biggest of the dinosaurs. At the least they might break a leg and give me even more of an advantage.

I wasn't exactly sure that this plan would work, but after weeks of thinking, I hadn't come up with anything better.

I kept thinking about it and in the meantime, spent a couple more weeks shoring up the closed end of the canyon. I found some mud near a swamp nearby and started carrying it over in the broken Pteranodon egg shells I had saved from my nest raids. They actually made pretty good buckets. I just kept dumping the buckets of mud over the edge. I hoped that when the mud dried it would form some kind of concrete holding the rocks and trees together. Who knew if this was going to work? I just needed my victim to stay trapped long enough to end its life.

Finally, the canyon and the path were completed to my satisfaction. I found some sturdy, thick branches that I placed underneath the boulders along the rim. I might need them to push the gigantic rocks over the edge. I was just about ready to take my big idea on a trial run. Just the thought of it would always get my blood pumping. Could I really do this? Could I turn the tables on these perfect hunting machines and transform them into the hunted. I was going to pull it off or die trying.

Finally, I had to figure out a way to lure the dinosaurs I would be hunting to the beginning of the path. I couldn't just scout around the valley hoping to run into one of them and then get them to chase me to the path. That would take way too much energy and would likely cause me to end up very, very dead. I had to find a way to lure them to the path, so I could get them to chase me from there. That was the only way this was going to work.

Again, I spent a few days thinking long and hard about animal behavior. One thing I knew for certain was that each of these vicious killers had something in common. Besides wanting to eat me for dinner, I mean. They all had an incredible sense of smell. Just a few minutes after every single bloody massacre, some other beast would show up to challenge the kill. Sometimes the fighting to protect the kill was more violent than the original battle. The biggest and baddest dinosaur always came out on top. The smaller carnivores would kill and eat as fast as they could because they knew it wouldn't be long before somebody else came along to steal their dinner.

So obviously they all had a keen sense of smell. When there was the scent of blood in the air it didn't take them long to track down where it was coming from. So, if I was going to lure them in, I was going to need some meat. And I was going to need to string it up high enough that the smaller carnivorous dinosaurs wouldn't be able to reach it.

I watched another kill from high above and waited a couple of days so the coast was clear before I went down to inspect it. Just as I had imagined, it was picked clean. Not a shred of meat was left anywhere. What the carnivores hadn't finished off, the birds and the insects had devoured. I did manage to salvage some of the skin, which came in pretty handy. I made myself a shirt and a couple of large pouches to carry stuff in. I figured they would probably be useful later. I also made something that kind of looked like a basket, but was open enough that the smell of the meat (if I ever found any) could make its way into the gigantic nostrils I was trying to attract.

I realized that I was probably going to have to take out a couple of Oviraptors to fill my basket. Again these guys were impossible to catch, hard to trap and even harder to kill even if you managed to get one in your snare. You couldn't spear them, or shoot them with a bow and arrow, because they always jumped away at the last second. Basically you just had to club them to death. Since they didn't have much meat and what they did have tasted horrible, I had given up on killing them and spent most of my time just swiping their eggs. They had sharp pointy teeth and a nasty disposition, so I really just tried to avoid them.

But since I didn't really have any other big ideas, I set out a bunch more snares and eventually I was able to get a couple of them to hold still long enough to club them to death. So, I took them, my basket trap and the rest of everything I thought I might need and headed back to the canyon. At the trail head I climbed high up in a tree, strung up the basket with the two dead oviraptors and headed back to my cave planning to come back the next day to see if my first victim had arrived.

I could barely sleep that night I was so excited. I left for the canyon even before the sun came up, but my plan had failed. At least sort of. Both the basket and the Oviraptors were gone, but there were some gigantic footprints in the mud underneath the trap. So, it look s like something was really interested in a free meal. That meant if it had any brains at all it would come back again to check find out if it could get lucky again. Perfect.

It was also clear that I needed to stay near or in the tree, if I wanted to be there during snack time. All I needed now was a couple more dead Oviraptors and I'd be ready to go. Hopefully, by this time next week I'll be writing all about the grilled dinosaur filet I had for dinner. Sweet.

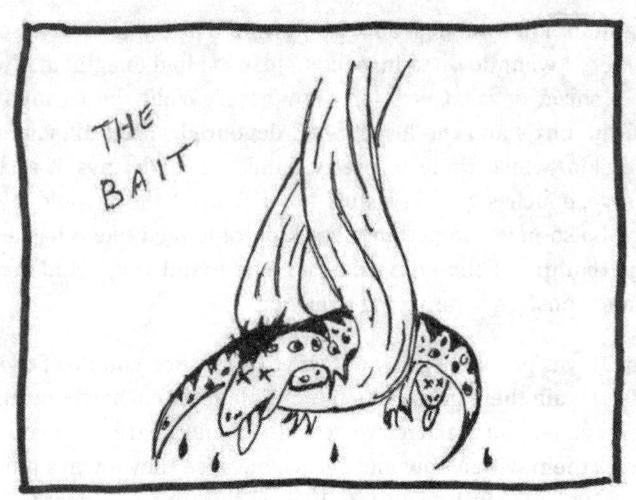

DAY 205 / WHAT CAN GO WRONG WILL GO WRONG

Today I almost died. Again.

It took me a few days to snare and kill the Oviraptors I needed to bait my trap. I marched back to the canyon and weaved my way up the trail to where my empty basket was still waiting in the tree. I shimmied up the tree and carefully positioned the fresh carcasses into the basket. I made certain that I sliced them open enough that the scent could easily be smelled. There was even a little bit of dino-blood dripping onto the ground far below. Yeah, that oughtta do it.

The next part was the hardest part. I'm not the most patient kid in the world, so after about five minutes of waiting in the crook of tree, I got really bored. Then I got even more bored. I tried to occupy my mind, by going over the details step by step of what my plan was once my prey arrived. Every detail was meticulously planned.

"Dad, I'm bored."

"Imagine that."

"Seriously, can we go?"

"We just got here."

"About five hours ago."

"Did you bring your book?"

"Why?"

"So you can read it. So you won't be bored. So you'll stop bugging me."

"Which book?"

"The one you are reading. The one I reminded you to bring."

"That book?"

"Yes."

"I left it in the car."

"So, go get it."

"The other car."

"Seriously?"

"Seriously."

"I've done all I could. It's not my job to entertain you."

"Can I borrow your phone?"

"Why?"

"So, I can play some games."

"I don't have any games."

"Yes, you do. I put them on there."

"Are you allowed to touch my phone?"

"Not usually."

"You're grounded."

"I'm bored..."

I'm not sure exactly when I dozed off, but I definitely woke up when the Velociraptors arrived and I fell out of the tree. As Dad might say: this was an "unmitigated disaster". The perfect combination of bad luck and stupidity. The bad luck was that instead of one somewhat manageable dinosaur, I had at least three to deal with. The stupidity was that on the most important day of my life I had somehow managed to drift off to sleep.

Team "V" must have smelled the dead Oviraptors and had come to inspect the free meal. They couldn't have been the same ones who had raided the trap before, because they weren't tall enough to reach it. I don't know if these were the same morons who burned down my tree house, but it didn't really matter, since the second I fell out of the tree they lost interest in the Oviraptors and were suddenly very fascinated with…you guessed it…yours truly.

I had the presence of mind to unsheathe my blade, but I already realized my big plan had absolutely no chance of succeeding. Not only were two of the Raptors blocking the trailhead, these guys were going to be a lot more agile, and getting away from all three of them was probably going to be impossible. The only good news was that I hadn't seemed to hurt myself falling out of the tree. I thought for a fleeting second about going back up the tree, but I knew they would just wait me out.

I acted instinctively. I leaped toward the closest Raptor jamming my blade deep into his leg. I figured if he couldn't run, then he couldn't catch me. I really don't think these beasts were used to smaller prey like me attacking them, so he definitely looked surprised. His scream must have prodded the other two into action, because now they were both coming towards me. Oh, wow. I leaped up onto a rock and then up a higher one. I only had a couple of seconds before they would be all over me. I dropped down off the rock just as the first Raptor arrived slashing his teeth toward me. I swiped my knife backwards, but I whiffed. I dropped and rolled under a fallen tree trunk just as Raptor number two arrived. He didn't take too kindly to my Leatherman as I drove it deep into his clawed foot. More screaming.

I glanced up and could see that the trailhead was just a short distance away. If I could somehow reach the beginning of the path, I might have a chance. Especially if two of the three Raptors were limping from my knife wounds. I sprinted toward the path dodging between two Raptors. They collided into each other with a thud, and this bought me a couple of precious moments. I was almost in the clear when the third Raptor shockingly leaped completely over me to block the path. These dingleberries weren't that bright, but they were such great athletes.

I immediately switched directions, but my path was blocked that way too. Drat. In a half second I was completely surrounded by the three Raptors. I crouched down and started swinging my blade back and forth constantly changing my position. Ninja Brett. They must have remembered that blade, because they definitely were giving it (and me) some well-earned respect. I couldn't defend this position for long though. Sooner or later one of them was going to make a move. My only hope was to bull-rush the weakest one and hope that I could slip by him before he ripped my head off.

I wiped off the bloody blade on my pants leg, picked out a Raptor and blindly rushed forward. When I opened my eyes I was clear of the Raptors, and these three dim-wits were staring at something up in the air. The thunderous roar above me just about burst my eardrums. It was like a sonic blast of sound and hot air at the same time. I looked up and saw the monstrous Tyrannosaurus rex looming over all three of the raptors and me. I hadn't seen a T. rex in the valley for weeks, but I'm guessing he was the one who had raided my trap. Now he was back.

Time stood still. One one-thousand, two one-thousand...then everything accelerated. The Raptors and I scattered like bowling pins in every direction. Out of the corner of my eye I saw him snap at one of the Raptors and rip his head off in mid-air. Oh my. I started running down the path, cutting and turning and running for my life. I was surprised to see one of the other Raptors ahead of me. He must have had the same idea. He didn't have to outrun the T. rex, he just had to outrun me.

The earth-pounding footsteps behind me were getting closer, but I knew we were almost to the canyon. Just keep going. The next thing happened so fast I'm not even sure I can describe it to you. I saw one Raptor going over the edge of the canyon ahead of me and heard him screaming when he realized he was airborne. I hit my vine swing just as the T. rex was rounding the last corner. The swing worked perfectly and I landed safely on the other side of the canyon. The T. rex must have been smarter than I thought because he pulled up skidding and snarling with just enough room to stop at the edge of the canyon. WOW!

My heart was pounding in my ears and eyes. He brought his massive body upright, roaring down into the canyon. I ducked behind a rock and hoped he hadn't seen me. I was shaking like a leaf. This guy meant business. When he realized that the Raptor was trapped in the canyon and he couldn't reach his meal, he went absolutely crazy. He paced up and down the canyon's edge trying to find a safe way down. Every few seconds he let out a horrible, booming bellow that echoed up and down the valley. I actually felt sorry for the Raptor. He was practically killing himself trying to run and jump and scramble up and out of the canyon rocks. Just like me, he was terrified.

Finally, after what seemed like hours, the T. rex gave up and went back to wherever he came from. I looked down at the Raptor. He was almost gone. Not only had he been injured from the flying fall into the canyon, he had worn himself out trying to escape. His breathing was shallow. I knew what I had to do. I found my narrow path down into the canyon, and with one swift stroke of my Leatherman I finished him off.

The grilled Raptor meat wasn't too bad, and I saved enough to bait my next trap. Now I knew that my plan had worked, and would work again. Not only was I going to be able to just survive, I was going to thrive in Cretaceous World. I wiped the dripping grease off my chin and smiled. I also realized that I was going to need more of an advantage when these monsters were chasing me. I would have to wound them while they were feeding on the bait to gain an advantage. Once I had the advantage, they would be mine. All mine. Awesome.

DAY 542 / UP, UP & AWAY

After I finally got the hang of hunting and killing the food I needed to eat to survive, I have to admit it finally got a little boring. Sure it was dangerous and exciting, but I discovered that if I smoked the meat it would last a really long time. I dug out some deep pits around my cave and covered them up really well with dino-skins. That made the meat last even longer, so I spent less and less time at the canyon and had more free time to explore. I kept venturing further and further into my lost world. I had to admit that dino jerky was pretty tasty and if I took enough in my Camelback I could go for a couple of days without having to return to my cave. I usually just found a big tree to sleep in.

Every once in a while I would think about my old home in Florida and my family. Occasionally I got lonely, but I was having so much fun learning how to survive that it didn't really bother me that much. I mean, seriously? Wasn't this the ultimate adventure for a ten-year old boy? I didn't even know if I was ten anymore. Was I getting older in this prehistoric world? I knew that I had been gone for about a year and half, but I didn't feel any different. My clothes were pretty much completely worn out, so I didn't wear them anymore. Whenever I needed something new to wear I just cut out some dino-skin and tried to make it fit the best I could. I still wore my hiking boots every now and then if I had a long way to hike, but mostly I just went barefoot. Swinging through the vines of my valley jungle, I probably looked a lot like Tarzan. Brett-of-the-jungle. I liked that.

What I really wanted to do was climb all the way up to the volcano and check that out. But that looked like it might take a week or two to go and come back. I was getting more confident in my survival skills, but I wasn't sure if I was ready to tackle that. I had to remind myself every day not to become careless. One stupid mistake and my dream world would come crashing down. I couldn't afford to get hurt or to get sick. And most of all I couldn't afford to get caught and eaten by one of the predators who periodically showed up in my valley to feed. But like I said, most of the time these big monsters made plenty of noise and announced their arrival long before you saw them.

What would be really cool would be if I could fly! Then I wouldn't need to worry about getting caught on the ground and I could soar up, up and away to the volcano and check out everything that was going on in this world. That's when I had my next brilliant idea. Awesome.

My valley was full of Pteranodons. Every day I could see them flying high in the thermals and nesting on the cliff walls. Unlike my earlier encounter with one, the Pteranodons didn't really seem to be interested in me or what I was doing. They appeared to feed mostly in the nearby lakes, and were basically harmless if I stayed out of their way. I occasionally swiped one of their eggs for an omelet or the shell, but I always waited until they were away from their massive nests.

Now Pteranodons aren't birds, they are dinosaurs. They didn't have feathers and they looked more like a flying reptile than a bird. When some of them landed they walked on four legs, not two. There seemed to be several different species: some were about the size of a bald eagle, but I had seen some that were as big as a small airplane. If I could somehow manage to capture and train one that size, I could fly anywhere for days.

I started thinking about how I could make this happen. There wasn't really any way I could capture one of the full grown ones, because they were just too big. One slap from that gigantic skull crest and I was dead meat. The smaller ones weren't large enough to be able to carry me. What I really needed was to kidnap one of the babies, bring it back down to the cave and train it to fly me while it was growing up. It was a crazy idea I know, but maybe I could make it work.

For the next few weeks I carefully observed the Pteranodons and scouted out their nest areas. They definitely didn't appreciate me snooping around, and let me know it with their horrendous squawking and flapping. I noticed that whenever they had babies, the mother guarded the nest area very jealously. They only left for short periods of time to feed or to bring back fish to the youngsters in the nest.

I found a suitable nest not too terribly far from my cave. It was a tough climb to get there, but not impossible. I patiently waited until the nest was unoccupied. I grabbed the edge of the nest and peeked over into the bottom. The smell of rotting fish was unmistakable. Yup, four perfect eggs. I left the four eggs intact and carefully made my way back to the cave and started thinking about my problem.

Once again I considered everything I knew about animal behavior. I was obviously going to have to wait until the eggs were hatched and probably a couple of weeks after that. That hatchling was going to have to be developed, and be able to see and walk if I was going to have any luck training it. I was also going to have to feed it and eventually build a harness to hang onto during flight. This was getting very complicated. I just decided to take it one step at a time. First I needed to capture my Pterosaur.

I spent a lot of time climbing up to the nest, and getting as close as I could without disturbing the mother. It seemed like she was getting used to me being nearby which could be awesome. Good thing she didn't know I was planning to kidnap one of her babies. It wasn't long until the eggs hatched, and I started thinking about how I was actually going to pull this off. The trick was going to be getting the baby back down the cliff without falling off the edge and smashing my brains out on the rocks below.

I figured I had about three weeks before the big day. I started working on making a knapsack that was big enough for me to put the baby in, but not so big that it would hinder me from climbing. I was pretty worried that the mother Pteranodon might attack me while I was coming back down. I was going to need to be able to hold onto the knapsack, climb and possibly fend off an attack all at the same time.

While I was sitting on the cliff one day thinking over my issues, I did a double take. There it was again. Smoke, far, far down in the valley. This time I wasn't able to convince myself it was just mist rising through the mid-morning air. No, that was definitely smoke. Hmmm...

Well, I didn't have time to spend the day or two it would take investigating it, because tomorrow was the Big Day. I went to bed early that night, so I could be up at dawn. I didn't know how long I would have to wait to swipe my flying machine. The sooner I got up there the better. Who knew what was going to happen? I had to be ready for anything and everything.

Unfortunately, when I got up the next morning it was raining pretty hard. Bad idea to go cliff- climbing in this kind of weather. I wasn't that stupid. I needed everything to be dry and clear if my plan was going to work. I hated waiting, but I spent the whole day in my cave going over my plan step by step, and I forgot all about the smoke in the valley.

I woke up the next day and everything was perfect. I tied up my hiking boots really tight, and strapped on my Leatherman. Next I double checked my Camelback making sure that I had food, water and duct tape. Finally I pulled the knapsack over my head and headed out of the cave. I was in high spirits as I started climbing, excited but nervous. It took me over an hour of steady climbing to reach the nest. By the time I got there the sun was fully up and the Pteranodons were swooping and soaring in the morning updrafts.

I got into position and took a couple of pulls of water to hydrate. This was going to be a hot one. Hopefully, I wasn't going to have to wait too long. I crept closer to the nest. No sign of mom anywhere. Maybe this was going to be easier than I thought. I wasn't going to have to create a distraction if she wasn't there defending her nest. I pulled myself up to the nest and looked over the edge. Wow – four perfect baby Pteranodons. They were actually kind of cute. Any one of them would be just fine. I took one last glance around, and when I didn't see anything, I made my move.

I scrambled over the edge, and dropped down into the nest. Again, this nest was bigger than any eagle's nest you've ever seen. It was basically the size of a small car, and stunk to high heaven. The smell of rotting fish and baby Pteranodon poop was almost enough to make me vomit. As soon as the babies saw me, they started going nuts. They either thought I had brought them food or that I was trying to eat them. At any rate, they started flapping and raising a ruckus that would have notified any mother Pteranodon within five miles. I had to move quickly.

I whipped off the knapsack and then the Camelback. I took out some scraps of meat from the Camelback and tossed them in the direction of the babies. That shut them up for a couple of seconds while they were greedily slurping them down. I realized that I hadn't brought nearly enough food. Stupid mistake. I picked out the baby I wanted and grabbed the duct tape. I ripped off a piece of tape and held it in my mouth, and then I dove for the closest one. I practically tackled him, but he was slippery. It took me a couple more attempts to finally get a hold of him and then the other babies went completely nutzoid. They were screaming and pecking at me with everything they had. It was mostly annoying, but I was worried they were going to hit one of my eyes and blind me. I took the tape I had between my teeth and wrapped it around my baby's snapping mouth. That at least stopped him for a second.

I was trying to be careful not to damage him, but he was fighting me every second. I grabbed the remaining roll of duct tape, and quickly wrapped some around and around his beak. Then I folded his wings and shoved him into my knapsack. I knew I was running out of time, but it was hard to move around in the uneven nest with other babies jumping all around and pecking me every chance they got. I slung my Camelback and the knapsack back over my shoulder and pulled myself up to the edge. Time to get the heck out of here!

The force of the mother's swinging crest almost knocked me out, and caused me to tumble back into the nest. Wow, was she ever unhappy. (Talk about an angry bird!)

Just for a few seconds, time stood still. The cold, black eyes that stared me down sent a chill down my spine. She must have known I was stealing one of her babies, and her maternal instincts were in full-blown defense mode. When she came at me, I did the best leg swing kick I knew how. This knocked her off balance for just the half second I needed. She snapped at me and barely missed, just as I rolled to other side of the nest. Unfortunately I was going to have to exit the nest on the opposite side from where I had come in. I scrambled up the inside of the nest and swung over the edge. I was hanging by some thick sticks in the nest, but by then she had recovered. WHERE WAS THE DARN WALL...?!?!

There she was above me shrieking and pecking at my hands. I tried to find a place for my feet, but I was just kicking in mid-air, flailing helplessly. I could feel the blood streaming down my arms from her incessant pecking, and I knew I couldn't hang on much longer. First my right hand came loose, and I was dangling by one arm above the two-hundred foot cliff. I desperately looked around for something to leap onto or to grab. The angry mother Pteranodon just kept shrieking and pecking on the hand that was still grasping the nest.

I let go and spun and twisted trying to grasp any root or small shrub that was growing out of the wall of the cliff. Falling, I somehow managed to find a small dried bush that started coming loose the second I grabbed it. Now the Pteranodon was out of her nest and on me again, flapping and screaming and pecking me all at the same time.

The roots of the dried out bush finally pulled out, and there I was again falling, falling, falling rocketing toward the bottom of the canyon.

DAY 627 / HOW TO TRAIN YOUR PTERANODON

Somehow I miraculously managed to survive the fall off the cliff. Of all the lucky things that have happened to me on this crazy adventure, that one had to be the luckiest. As I was falling I just closed my eyes and waited for the end to come with my brains and body being splattered all over the canyon floor. I never realized this until later, but the cliff slightly curved as it went up toward the sky. So as I was falling I begin bouncing off the cliff wall as I fell down.

This must have slowed me down just a little bit, and fortunately I never hit my head as I was hurtling toward my certain death. Then I hit a few more bushes and roots growing out of the cliff slowing me down even more. Right before I got to the bottom I started hitting the higher branches of one of the big leafy trees that grew along the valley right next to the cliff. Smack, bang, oooff. The branches were killing me, but they were actually slowing me down. I hit one of the bigger ones really hard and I think that's when I broke my leg and finally blacked out from the pain.

I finally came to when I felt the baby Pteranodon squirming and kicking in the knapsack. I was lying face-up in the big, leafy branches of a huge tree. My left leg was on fire, but I was still alive. A miracle. Unbelievable. And AWESOME!

I won't bore you with all the painful details, but I somehow managed to get down from the tree, made myself a splint, and crawled and hobbled the long, grueling way back to my cave. I passed out a couple of times from the pain, but I finally got back and amazingly still had my baby Pteranodon. Alive. When I finally dragged myself back into my cave I was exhausted. I managed to tether my captive baby dino to a rock, and then I must have slept for at least twenty-four hours.

I finally awoke to the sound of the Pteranodon crying for food. He must have gnawed his way through the duct tape. Poor little guy was starving, and crying for his mama. I tossed him some of my dino jerky from my Camelback, and that shut him up for a little while. Good to know that he was so responsive to food. Then I ate a little for myself (I was starving) and drank my fill of the water. I assessed my situation, and figured that once again I had avoided death and was going to survive.

I crawled around to see if I could make myself a better splint. I wasn't exactly sure my leg was broken, but I knew that I was going to have to stay close to the cave for a few weeks while I healed up. I finally made myself a more effective splint out of some branches and vines, and after a couple of days I was finally able to hobble around. I found a thick, sturdy branch to use as a cane. I was going to survive.

I decided to name my new pet, "Skinny". Unlike his very angry mother, he seemed to take a shine to me almost right away. Probably because I was feeding him. I had read where young animals make an "imprint" on whoever is taking care of them. I was hoping that would make Skinny easier to train.

Well that idea seemed to work, because after a couple of weeks of feeding Skinny, I was able to release him from his tether. He followed me around everywhere I went in the cave, just like a faithful dog. I knew that he was a wild animal and would never be completely domesticated, but I decided to worry about that later. It was really nice having a companion after all these months of being alone and on my own. We were hitting it off.

I finally started getting better, and was able to get around without my cane. I don't know if my leg was broken or just seriously sprained, but every day I was moving better and getting stronger. Skinny was getting stronger and bigger as well. He had already grown to about twice the size he was when I had "adopted" him. Eventually I knew that he would get too big to hang in the cave with me, but we could cross that bridge when we came to it.

I figured it was time to start his training. He would be mature enough to fly soon – he was already hopping and flapping his wings and getting airborne for a few feet at a time. It was fun to watch him learn how to use his wings. He seemed to be getting bigger every day. Fortunately I had plenty of food stored up from my previous kills. I even managed to catch a few fish for him out of the waterfall lagoon. They were too bony for me to eat, but he really loved them. I knew that eventually he would have to find his own food, but for now we were good.

The first thing I taught him to do was respond to my whistle. This was probably the easiest thing I taught him. I would whistle, Skinny would come and then I would reward him with a small fish or some dino-jerky. The next step was getting him used to the harness I had made out of the skins I had left over from my kills. I had plenty of that stuff, and it was both supple and strong. I experimented with several different styles and types. He didn't really like them at first, but eventually he got used to one of the lighter ones, and practically wore it all the time without any problems. The only issue was that whenever he got really rambunctious, it would slip off and fall around to his belly. I needed to fix that if I was ever going to get airborne.

The next thing was to get Skinny used to actual flying. All this training wasn't going to do any good if he spent his whole life just hopping and flapping from place to place. I tried everything I knew to try to get him to fly, but he seemed perfectly content following me around, eating up all my food and just hanging out. It was great having a buddy to pal around with, but what I really wanted was to fly. Besides I knew if he didn't learn to fly, he would eventually get stalked and eaten by one of the many carnivores who came to our valley on a regular basis. He wasn't fast enough to outrun them, and he was getting so big I knew I couldn't hide him in the cave much longer.

I even tried flying him like a kite. I found the longest vine I could, and cut it down. Then I tied it to his harness and took him down to some open areas below the waterfalls. We must have looked pretty funny with me running as fast as I could and him hopping and squawking behind me. We both ended up in heap of dust and skinned-up knees. He didn't understand. No matter what I tried, he just wouldn't flap his wings hard enough to get up into the air. I pointed up in the air at all the Pteranodons flying in the distance.

"See, that Skinny? That could be us! We could be flying up there with those guys. Come on, fella, FLY!"

He just tilted his head at me quizzically and let out a pathetic squawk.

"No, you don't get a fish. Nice try, junior."

Desperate times call for desperate measures. It was time for Skinny to let his instincts take over, and fly like the mighty dinosaur that he was. Early one morning I grabbed Skinny by the tether, and half dragged him up the cliffs as far as I could go without him knocking me off. He was obviously not enjoying our little adventure.

I knew this might be the last time I ever saw him. If he didn't fly, he would surely be smashed to bits on the rocks below. If he did fly the chances were pretty good that he'd never come back again. I grabbed him the best I could, and whispered in his ear.

"This is it, little fella. You have to learn to fly or you will never be able to survive in this prehistoric world. I'm sorry that we have to go through this, and

I'm sorry that I can't show you how to do it. But I know that you know how to do this. It's in your genes and your DNA. YOU CAN DO THIS...YOU WERE BORN TO FLY...!!!"

If Pteranodons can looked puzzled, Skinny definitely looked it as I shoved him backwards off the cliff and into the open sky. My heart sank as he dropped like a stone and quickly disappeared squawking and screeching into the valley below. I watched him until I couldn't see him anymore. I whistled and waited. Nothing. I waited a few more minutes. More nothing.

I was crushed. I had killed my only companion in this violent world. Skinny had trusted me and I had betrayed him. I guess I had forgotten how to cry, so I was surprised when the tears started flowing and the snot came pouring out of my nose. I sat there blubbering for a few minutes feeling sorry for myself, until I finally got control and I stopped sobbing. It wasn't going to do any good to sit here and cry like a baby. I got myself turned around and started the lonely descent down the cliff. I decided to give Skinny one last farewell whistle as I made my way down. It was kind of pathetic since I was still all choked up.

What was that? When I heard the screeching behind me, I just about fell off the cliff. I whipped my head around just in time to see Skinny fold up his wings and go into a head-long dive towards the valley. Not only was he flying, he was showing off for me. He was amazing.

WOOOOOOOOOOOOOHOOOOOOOOOO...!!!!!!

So, I had been right all along. I shook my head in amazement. Skinny's instincts had taken over and he had finally learned how to fly. I watched him soar and dive in the thermals over and over again. He looked like he belonged up in the sky. He was majestic. I whistled and whistled for him until I couldn't whistle anymore, but he was having too much fun trying out his broad wings. I was tingling all over and was as happy as I'd ever been in my whole life. I just wondered if he'd ever come back to me. Oh well, at least he had learned to fly even if I never could. Mission accomplished. Awesome!

DAY 701 / FIRE ON THE MOUNTAIN, LIGHTNING IN THE SKY

All I can say is flying a dinosaur is the most awesome, incredible, amazing thing that has ever happened to me. It's better than playing video games for days at a time, it's better than the "best Christmas ever" (Dad says that EVERY year), and it's even better than going to Opening Day of the baseball season. It's just better than anything you could ever imagine. And then some.

Yeah, it took a lot of trial and error to get Skinny used to me flying on his back, but eventually we figured it out. We had multiple falls, skinned knees, bumps on his head and mine, problems with the harness, a couple of really scary near misses and a few scrapes with some other aggressive not-very-friendly Pteranodons. After a few weeks of working with Skinny every single day almost all day long, he finally got used to the idea of me riding on his back while he was flying. It probably helped that he had never really gotten completely used to flying by himself.

So if Skinny was my uglier, thinner version of "Puff the Magic Dragon", I guess that made me "Jackie Paper." We got better and better at working together, and took longer and longer flights. Taking off and landing were the toughest parts. Once we got up in the air we were a great team. He even learned to respond to my knees pressing into his flanks to turn, so I didn't even need to use the harness much at all.

We finally got to the point where our takeoffs and landings were almost smooth. I found a somewhat level place, and spent a couple of days clearing out the rocks and boulders. I uprooted most of the bushes. Then we tromped and stomped back and forth until our landing strip was almost flat. It had a slight downward slope, so I would let Skinny get a head start and then I would jump on his back as he lifted off. That way he didn't have to carry my weight from a dead stop. I missed his back a few times and slid off a few more times, but the more we practiced the better we got at it. I hoped that as he got older and filled out a little more he would get stronger and be able to take off without me having to jump onto his back while he was on the run.

Skinny and I were just about out of food, so I decided to try something different with my next hunt. We had been practicing our banking and turning, and Skinny was getting really agile. He could practically stop in mid-air (at least for a few seconds) and turn on a dime. It was time for a predator hunt...from the air.

I caught a couple of the oviraptors and flew back to the canyon to bait the trap. What used to take over an hour now only took about five minutes. Yeah, air travel was definitely the way to go in this world. I checked out my path and made certain I had the boulders in place along the edge of the canyon for the kill if I needed them. Then instead of waiting in the tree near the trap, like I had been doing all along, we flew back to the cave. I signaled Skinny to wait for me there, and then I climbed high up on the cliffs where I had a clear view of the canyon, the path and my trap.

Sure enough it didn't take long until a hungry dino was gnawing on the dead oviraptors. From a distance I couldn't really identify the species, but it didn't look like anything I had seen before. It had a large crest on its head and was deep purple in color, almost black. This could be fun. I whistled for Skinny and within seconds he was beside me on a broad ledge on the cliff wall. I jumped on his back and we dropped off the wall, and sped toward the canyon. Just like in the movies.

We got to the canyon and the path in a matter of minutes. Just as I suspected, this was a completely different dinosaur that I had never seen before. From the looks of things he was pretty aggressive and was packing plenty of meat. Perfect. I wondered if he had ever been attacked by a hunter on a Pteranodon before?!?

Evidently not, because he had a very surprised look on his face when I banked Skinny toward him, and started screaming to get his attention. The remaining dead Oviraptor dropped out of his mouth and he turned his head, roaring as we buzzed by. As you know most of these humongous suckers have tiny, little baby arms that didn't do them much good. No wonder they had gone extinct. If you stayed away from their crushing, powerful jaws and their massive tails you were probably going to be okay.

I made a wide turn with Skinny, unsheathed my blade and headed back towards the purple dinosaur. Big Barney never saw me coming and when I slashed a big cut right between his shoulder blades, he roared in pain. I glanced back to see dino blood spurting like a geyser into the air, so I knew I must have hit an artery or something really big. Awesome.

I pulled Skinny into a mid-air stop, making sure the injured dinosaur got a good look at me. He fell for it, and started clomping, and chomping, and slobbering toward us. I wondered how long he would last with all that blood squirting everywhere. This was going to be so much easier than being chased on foot. Sure enough Big Barney's instincts got the better of him. He followed us blindly down the path, oblivious to the doom that awaited him. We kept flying back behind him, twisting and turning him in every direction. He was madder than a wet hornet.

He was close enough for me to hear his snapping teeth and for me to smell his foul breath, but Skinny was magnificent. It was like he knew exactly what to do. By the time we got the unidentified dinosaur to the canyon's edge, Barney was completely disoriented and exhausted. I hovered right beside him, he snapped at us a couple more times, then teetered on the edge and fell into the canyon – a nearly dead heap o' dino dinner. Thankfully, he must have broken his neck with the fall. I saw him twitch a couple of times and that was it.

Skinny and I watched him from the edge for a couple of minutes just to make sure he was a goner, but this was "game over". We flew down and I stripped as much meat as I could, and then we got out of there. I was able to come back several times with Skinny to reload my knapsack. By the time the smaller predators were swarming down the canyon walls, we had enough meat to last both of us for months. I planned to go back and take whatever skin was left after the scavengers had stripped off all the meat.

As Skinny and I enjoyed a delicious meal of fresh dinosaur steak, I watched the sun set over my valley. Things couldn't have been any better. Of course you know, just as soon as you start thinking that, something horrible is right around the corner.

Skinny and I spent our days exploring our world. He could fly for hours, so we just went wherever I felt like going. We flew up to the volcano and watched the hot lava rolling down the mountain. We even flew over the volcano and looked down into the boiling stew of magma and rock. The smell of sulfur was so strong it almost knocked me out. I was terrified to stay up here for long, and Skinny didn't like it either. This was way higher than any of his buddies ever came, and every now and then a big blast of rock, lava and steam would shoot into the air above the volcano. That was enough for me. If we got hit with one of those, it would be over in a second.

I wheeled Skinny around and we headed back. I thought about landing on the side of the volcano, but I just didn't know how hot the ground was there. Besides, there was nothing there for us above the tree line except cooling lava. The landscape was as barren as the surface of the moon. We dodged a lightning storm on the way home. What fun!

We soared over the volcano one day and flew all the way to the ocean. We landed on the beach, and we watched agile Plesiosaurs playing out in the ocean. I knew from my dinosaur history that all kinds of strange and mysterious (not to mention dangerous) creatures were lurking under the surface of the blue sea stretching out in front of me. Since I was so unfamiliar with this part of whatever continent I was on, we didn't stay for long. There was plenty of time to come back and explore later.

I saw the smoke again yesterday. It was unmistakable. Something or someone (?) was lighting fires in my valley. It was past time to find out what was going on. I filled up my Camelback, called for Skinny and we headed in the direction of what had to be a camp fire. What else could cause that smoke?

I heard the distinct roar of a Tyrannosaurus rex long before I got to the fire. He came into view in the distance, and it was obvious he had some poor creature on the run. I never knew which T. rex was which, but this guy looked particularly familiar. I was almost certain it was the same one who had chased me near the canyon a few months back.

I probably should have minded my own business and let nature take its course, but curiosity got the better of me. Skinny and I rapidly approached the massive, bouncing beast from behind. He was in full pursuit of something. When I got closer I heard the screaming. WHAT THE...?!?! I just about fell off my flying dinosaur when I saw the limp, lifeless body of my sister, Natalie, dangling out of the Rex's mouth. Not far away on the ground I saw my other sister, Maddie, standing her ground, howling helplessly into the prehistoric air. Not awesome.

DAY 710 / TWISTED SISTER

It's easy to write about it now, but at the time I had no plan, no clue, no earthly idea of what to do next. Just like the dinosaurs that I had to deal with on a daily basis, I was acting purely out of instinct. Seeing my two sisters after all this time was a complete and total shock, but seeing Natalie hanging out of the mouth of the most fearsome predator in all of natural history put me instantly in fight mode. I didn't know her status exactly, but I was going after her DEAD OR ALIVE.

I had spent most of my time avoiding T. rex. The only encounters I experienced were bad ones. Tyrannosaurs were the undisputed kings of this world. Nobody messed with these bad boys. When one of them came stomping and ripping through the valley everything headed for cover, including me. So now I was going against every instinct in my body. Come on Brett...just another dino with a big body and a tiny little brain...GAME ON...!!!

When I pulled Skinny up to a dead mid-air stop, I could feel his body trembling beneath me. He knew exactly what we were up against and he absolutely wanted no part of it. I leaned in, gave him a pat, and whispered in his ear. After our mid-air stop and turn, both the T. rex and Maddie must have seen us at the same time. The look on Maddie's face was priceless. Talk about shock and awe!

The best I could hope for was to get the beast to drop Natalie and go for me. For that to happen I was going to have to get close enough to distract him. I buzzed by him as close as possible. Close enough to see that maybe, just maybe Natalie was still alive. Out of the corner of my eye I saw Mads loading up what had to be a sling. Oh yeah, Maddie, had a lot of experience getting out of these kinds of jams.

The Rex was confused. He obviously wasn't used to being harassed by a flying kid on a Pteranodon. I spurred Skinny higher and he folded his wings as we sped toward Big Boy. This time we swooped in even closer and I slashed toward the Rex's eye with my Leatherman. I just missed but took a big slice right below his eye. I had miscalculated though, and the impact of the knife with the tough hide threw both me and Skinny off balance. I desperately fought to hold my position, but my saddle was slowly slipping around to Skinny's belly. Skinny was flapping and trying to right himself, but he couldn't hold the center.

As I slipped all the way to Skinny's underbelly, he almost righted himself. But he overcompensated, and we lurched back in the other direction. By this time I was scraping the ground and ripping my back to shreds on the rocks and bushes on the ground. It was a miracle that I didn't hit my head. I pulled myself up as tight as I could to Skinny's stomach. Skinny fought to keep us airborne, but by now it was too late. We went skidding and sprawling into a big pile of rocks. Ouch...FUDGE!!!

I could hear Rexy stomping toward us. Through the cloud of dust I saw Maddie step forward and ferociously hurl her sling shot through the air. I heard the boulder whistle by me as it spun through the air. I was disoriented from the crash and could barely see, but it looked like Mads scored a direct hit right into the now bloody eye of Tyrannosaurus rex.

"NICE shot, Maggie!"

No time for a conversation now. The Rex screamed and simultaneously flipped Natalie up in the air at the same time. No way was he giving up this easily. Natalie must have still been alive, because I saw her reach out and grab her captor by the neck. Now he was really engaged. He ignored us for the time being and started throwing his head around like a bucking bronco trying to shake Nat loose.

"HANG ON NATALIE!!!!"

I found my knife on the ground and ran straight for this Cretaceous sister killer. I aimed for his soft underbelly. I was hoping to hit a vital organ, but my adrenaline was pumping so hard, I just wanted to inflict some serious pain on this monster. I leaped, stabbed and screamed at the same time. I must have been really flying because the blade, my hand and half my arm sunk all the way into his stinking dino guts. He instantly stopped worrying about Natalie, and gave me his full attention. Unfortunately my arm was stuck and I was tugging as hard as I could trying to pull it out. I saw Maddie step forward with another big ol' rock loaded and ready. Hallelujah! We were in the fight of our lives, but we were giving this prehistoric monster all he wanted. Can you feel us now, Big Fella?!?!

My arm came free when the T. rex ripped me out with his massive jaws and flipped me about forty feet in the air. The hard landing knocked the breath out of me and I doubled over in agony. That's how I lost my knife, and cracked about six ribs. I almost blacked out from the pain, but I was still conscious enough to see Maddie was in trouble. Her rock must have missed or done very little damage. Poor Natalie was barely hanging on by one arm, and the enraged Rex was after Maddie. She was running right towards me with a look of pure terror on her face.

I finally caught my breath and I saw what had to be our last hope. Out of the now gaping wound I had inflicted on the T. rex some of his intestines were dragging on the ground. Blood and guts and gore were pouring out of him. Direct hit! We just had to hang on for a few more minutes and he'd be done for. I grabbed for Maddie as she was running by. The bloody, furious Rex was right on us.

"THIS WAY!!!"

Just then Skinny, who miraculously was not hurt by our crash, suddenly swooped in behind us and pulled up mid-flight right in the face of our nemesis flapping his wings and distracting him. Way to go, Boy! This gave us the three seconds we needed to jump up on a huge boulder. My broken ribs were killing me. I whistled for Skinny and he turned just in time to miss the powerful snapping jaws of the Rex. The massive dinosaur was staggering around and wasn't going to last much longer. I was worried that he was going to fall and smash Natalie (still barely hanging on) to smithereens.

"HANG ON, MADDIE…!!!"

I swiftly tightened up the saddle and swung up on Skinny's back, and Maddie grinned from ear to ear. I grabbed her arm and pulled her on behind me.

"Brett, this is CRAZY…but AMAZING!"

I was worried Skinny didn't have enough strength left to fly off the boulder from a dead stop with both of us on him, but I guess he was just as pumped up as the rest of us. We lifted off straight up into the air, and I pulled the reins directly toward the now tottering T. rex. Natalie looked like she might be unconscious again, but she was somehow still holding on.

The T. rex saw us coming right at him, and this must have revived him. With half of his guts strewn out all over the ground it was incredible that he was still standing. He summoned his strength and stood up to his full height. He leaped, turning and snapping at us and prevented us from grabbing Nat. He just missed us and we could feel his hot, dying breath on our faces. I banked and wheeled Skinny just in time to see him gasping and stumbling and falling.

"GRAB NATALIE!!!!"

We got there just as the massive seven-ton dino was about to smash into the ground. Natalie was now barely clinging to the front of his neck as he was falling to the earth. Skinny swooped underneath the doomed T. rex, and Maddie reached out and snatched Natalie just before he landed with a thunderous, earth-shaking thud. Skinny struggled to stay in the air with all the extra added weight, but he finally pulled us up and we gradually ascended up, up and away towards my cave.

"Oh, wow."

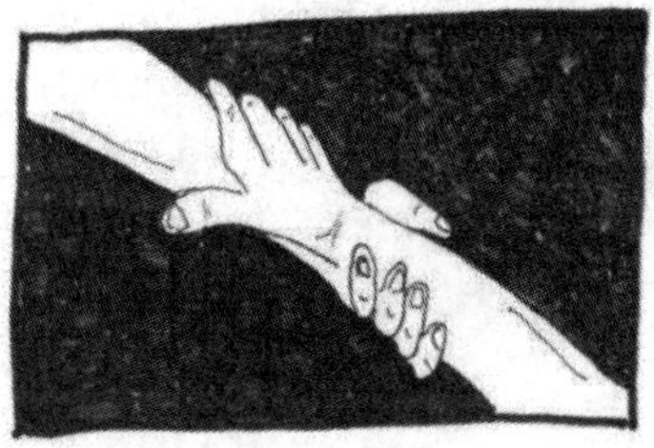

DAY 740 / GOOD TALK

It took several weeks for both Natalie and me to recover. But mostly Natalie. Maddie nursed us each back to health. First she had to pick and scrape all the rocks and gravel out of my back and wrap up my ribs, but then we turned our attention to Natalie. She was badly bruised and beaten from our battle with Thunder Lizard, but she didn't seem to have any broken bones. She must have caught some weird disease from the monster though, because she was running a high fever and kept fading in and out of consciousness. Maddie watched over her just about every second. I kept everyone supplied with plenty of food and water. Maddie told me their story.

"Brett, Natalie saved my life. If it wasn't for her I would be dead right now. Just a big pile of T. rex poop."

"What happened?"

"We got caught out in the open, and we were running for our lives to get away from that horrible creature."

"And...?"

Maddie took a deep breath and fought back the tears.

"And then I tripped and fell over some stupid rock or something."

"Yeah, we've got PLENTY of those here in the valley."

"So, I must have been tangled up in something, because I couldn't get up. Just as he was about to snap me up, Natalie jumped in between us."

"Oh, wow..."

"Wow is right. I finally twisted free, but by then he was already by me. And Natalie was in his mouth. I hate to even talk about it. I scrambled to my feet, but I had no idea how to save Nat. Fortunately, that's when you showed up."

"I saw the fire."

"Lucky for us."

"Yeah, you guys look like you've had a pretty rough go of it. Like a couple of starving rats."

"Thanks...we've been surviving on nothing but roots and berries almost since we got here. So when did you become big, bad King of Dinosaur Land?"

"It's been really weird. I've made a ton of mistakes, but somehow I've managed to survive in this crazy place."

"I didn't even recognize you. You look really...different. Leaner. Meaner."

"Well, I don't feel any different, but a lot has happened since I fell in the river."

"So, tell me about it. Sounds like you've had a wild adventure."

I took about two hours and told her about everything. About hiking in the Grand Canyon with Dad, about the marker, falling in the Colorado River and waking up in the Cretaceous Period.

"So, how do you know we are in the Cretaceous Era?"

"We have to be. All the dinosaur species I've been able to clearly identify seem to indicate we are in the late Cretaceous Period: T. rex, Triceratops, Pterosaurs, etc."

"What exactly is a Pterosaur?"

"You flew one here. Skinny is a Pterosaur."

"You trained a Pterosaur how to fly?!?"

"Well, technically he already knew how fly. I just taught him how to fly with me riding on his back. It was actually pretty easy. I could teach you guys how to do it."

"Incredible." It felt really weird having Maddie give me so many compliments. Usually we just bicker and fight whenever we are together.

Then I told her all about my tree house disaster, and how I had finally found the waterfall and the valley stretched out below us. I told her all about the canyon, and how I learned to hunt and kill dinosaurs. How I had stolen Skinny and taught him and me how to fly. She just kept shaking her head in amazement. I told her how I kept seeing the fires and wondering who or what was causing them.

"It's really cool that you guys learned how to start a fire. It took me almost forever to get mine going, and I have to be really careful to make sure it never goes out. Fire is one of the few things these dinosaurs are all afraid of."

Maddie started digging around in her pockets. She had a huge grin on her face as she tossed me something.

"Here, this should make your life a just a little bit easier."

I stared at the lighter she had tossed me. I laughed out loud. What an amazing little piece of technology from the modern world, which I had all but forgotten about. She was right. This was going to come in handy.

"So, tell me your story. What in the holy heck are you and Natalie doing here and how did you guys figure out I was here?"

"We DIDN'T know you were here. We were only hoping and guessing. We had given up on trying to find you, and were just trying to survive long enough to figure out how to get back home. It was a mistake to come here. We've almost been killed a dozen times."

"Tell me about it. This place is full of danger. How did you get here?"

"Sit down and take a load off. This is going to take a while."

I grabbed some dino jerky and took a seat in my hammock, swinging gently back and forth.

"Ready when you are, Mads."

"When Dad flew back from the Grand Canyon, obviously you weren't with him. When we asked him where you were, he said you had stayed an extra week to go to "Rock Climbing School." Sure Dad, whatever. Natalie got VERY worried, and we went through Dad's stuff and found the half used purple marker. We both knew that you must have used the marker and were trapped back in time somewhere. I was ready to use the marker right away, but Natalie had the really good idea that we should take a couple of days and PLAN. Since we had both been on these crazy time-traveling trips, we tried to think about some things we wished we had taken with us.

We gathered everything we thought might be helpful, and sat down to draw. We tried to think about where you might have gone in history: back to the invention of baseball, the first video games, World War II, the Titanic, Ice Age, Gold Rush...? Then Natalie reminded me you had been obsessed with dinosaurs since you were two years old. We agreed to try and draw a dinosaur. We got out one of your three-thousand books about dinosaurs and started drawing. We got in this really big argument about who was going to draw, since Natalie thinks SHE'S the artist in the family when everyone know it's me. We were both pulling on the marker, and all the ink spilled out. We thought we had ruined it, but then the markers worked their magic and then BAM BAM BAM the next thing you know we are running for our lives from stupid, gigantic, people-eating lizards. I think we've been here for about six months, but I really don't know exactly. Most of the stuff we brought with us to survive has been used or lost. I hate this place. It's horrible."

"It's not that bad once you figure out how to survive. Then it's actually cool. VERY cool."

"What's cool about having gigantic, slobbering, idiot predators trying to rip your head off every single second of every day?!?"

"You just have to learn to stay out of their way. Now that we are all together, I'm going to teach you guys how to learn to love Pangea."

"Pangea?"

"Yeah, I think that's where we might be...unless it's already broken up into continents. Who knows?"

"That would be awesome, but what we really need to do is find the bead and get home. I could really use a shower. And by the way, so could you."

I guess the compliments were over. "The bead?"

"Yup. On all these journeys you can't get home without finding the bead."

"Ok. Hey, it looks like Natalie is doing a little better..."

I didn't say anything else, but I had absolutely ZERO interest in going home. As far as I was concerned this was my "home". I loved everything about my world, and I had no intention of leaving it. I didn't care what they did, but I was as happy as I could be. I had taken my last shower. And my last piano lesson.

DAY WHATEVER / SAME SONG, SECOND VERSE, LITTLE BIT LOUDER, LITTLE BIT WORSE

Natalie eventually got all better, and everyone settled into living in my world. I flew Skinny back to the scene of the big battle, and after a lot of hunting and digging around eventually found my Leatherman. I showed the girls how I kept the blade in shape by sharpening it on a rock. I taught them all my survival tricks and they even showed me a few things they had learned. They were very excited to be able to eat meat for a change, and Natalie took over most of the cooking. We had plenty to eat and most things went smoothly. I even stopped constantly worrying about the fire, since we had the lighter now. Hopefully the lighter would last for a good, long time. Maddie showed me how she made her sling, and we all got pretty good at pegging the nosy Oviraptors that occasionally showed up trying to steal our food.

The days rolled into weeks, the weeks melted into months and I finally stopped keeping track of how long I had been here. It just didn't seem to matter anymore. I even captured a couple more baby Pteranodons and eventually taught Maddie and Natalie how to fly. We flew all over Pangea and saw incredible sights: herds of Brachiosaurs roaming over vast fields of long, tall grass, Plesiosaurs frolicking in the deep blue ocean, duck-billed Hadrosaurs half-submerged in crystal, clear lakes feeding their young. Every day was full of adventure. Sure we were stuck in the cave for days at a time when the massive thunderstorms passed through, but Natalie made up some fun games to play so it always went by quickly.

Everything was just about perfect except for this discussion we had on a regular basis.

Maddie: Brett don't you think it's about time that we thought about heading back to civilization?

Natalie: Yeah, I think I've enjoyed just about as much Albertosaurus steak as I can stand. I'm ready for some chicken fingers and french fries. With lots of ketchup.

Brett: Not happening. We have everything we are ever going to need right here.

Maddie: Well, maybe we should talk about it.

Natalie: And a brownie.

Brett: There's nothing to talk about.

Natalie: With ice cream.

Maddie: You're crazy, Brett. We need to decide what we should do.

Brett: I've already made up my mind. Why would you ever want to go back to the modern world?!? All those people. All those cars. All that pollution. All that noise. Bleh.

Natalie: And chocolate fudge with whipped cream and sprinkles.

Maddie: Well, I want to go to college. I want to grow up and have my own family. Have you noticed that we never change here? That we are stuck, lost somewhere in time. Don't you want to drive a car or have a career or get married?

Brett: Seriously?

Natalie: How about play video games for days on end?

Maddie: Or watch tv? Or go to the movies? Or read a book? Or have a cupcake?

Brett: You know what's really weird? I thought I would really miss those things, but I almost never think about them anymore. We never run out of things to do here. I never get bored.

Natalie: What about Mom and Dad?

Brett: Who?

Maddie: Ok, how about Buster?

Brett: Ok, I admit I miss Buster every now and then, but Skinny is almost like a pet. PLUS he can fly. All Buster does is chase his ball and look cute.

Natalie: I miss my friends. I miss going to school and playing softball. I miss practicing the piano.

Brett: You are a complete idiot.

Natalie: I'm just going to have to use my mind control on you.

Brett: Yeah, that works great on everything except your own mind.

Maddie: Stop bickering. We have to find the magic bead and get back home. We can't just stay here suspended in time forever.

Remember? The "magic beads" were the way Maddie and Natalie got back from their time-traveling adventures. Evidently it contained some of the same liquid that floated in the glass part of the pens. According to them when you swallowed the bead you ended up pretty much where you started from.

Brett: Why not? There's nothing stopping us.

Maddie: You already know the answer to that.

Brett: No, I don't. Please enlighten me, oh wise one.

Natalie. Brett, der. Ever notice we didn't have any dinosaurs roaming around our neighborhood back in Florida?

Brett: Besides Dad in his boxer shorts, you mean? What's your point?

Maddie: Her point is that this world is GOING TO END. It's not going to last forever. Dinosaurs became extinct for a reason.

Brett: Yeah, but nobody really knows exactly what got them.

Natalie: What difference does that make, dipwad? They became extinct.

Brett: Well, DIPTHONG, that could be millions of years from now.

Maddie: So we are just going to wait around here for millions of years waiting for some unknown disaster to strike? Or worse yet, to be eaten alive by some horrible predator?

Brett: That's never going to happen. We are safe in this cave.

Natalie: Brett it almost DID happen. Maybe you think it's fun to be mauled by a T. rex, but I can assure you it's NOT.

Maddie: Besides this world could end tomorrow. You don't know when disaster is going to happen.

Brett: So what? That's true for the modern world as well. Disaster can happen at any time. Or anywhere. You could get some nasty disease, or squashed by a car. There are fires and floods and hurricanes. You could get struck by lightning. You could get bitten by a poisonous snake or a spider.

Natalie: I hate spiders.

Maddie: Well if any of those things happen, don't you think it would be nice to have a doctor or a hospital close by. We don't even have a single Band-Aid here anymore.

Brett: We just need to be careful, that's all.

Natalie: But we AREN'T careful, Brett. We fly dinosaurs, we hunt the most vicious killers in the history of the animal kingdom, and we take incredible risks almost on a daily basis. Heck, you never even wash your hands before you scarf down your meals.

Maddie: Disgusting little piggy.

Brett: None of this matters anyway. We aren't going anywhere until one of you guys finds your precious, little beads. You can't fool me. I know you have been looking all over the place.

Natalie: That's right. We are more than ready to go back home.

Brett: This IS my home. Even if you find one, I'm not going anywhere. Not now, not ever.

Maddie: I bet you know where the bead is, but you are just not telling us.

Brett: You think that I need to keep you guys around? Did it look like I was having any problems whatsoever before you got here?

Natalie: Ok, fair enough. But we need you to help us find the bead. You know this world better than we do.

Brett: Whatever. Find it yourself.

Maddie: Whatever.

Natalie: What-evuh. But I would really love a banana. Is that too much to ask? Or maybe some waffles with strawberries and syrup.

Maddie: The maple kind?!?

I knew they were pretty frustrated with me, so I finally shut up. I had to secretly admit that I liked having them around. Most of the time we all got along great, and it was fun having human beings to hang around with. Even if it was my dopey sisters. Of course, I would never admit that to them. Plus it was kind of fun looking all over the place for a "magic bead" that we didn't even know if it existed or not. Once in a while I would pretend to help them look for it just to keep them from bugging me.

Maddie: Brett, do you feel that?

Brett: What?

Maddie: That.

Brett: So?

Maddie: That's the earth moving.

Brett: Happens about three times a week.

Natalie: Oh. I thought it was my stomach rumbling.

Maddie: Brett, that's the volcano.

Brett: I know that.

Maddie: Have you noticed the tremors are getting more powerful and more frequent?

Brett: No, as a matter of fact, I haven't.

Natalie: I have.

Brett: Big deal.

Maddie: Yes, Brett, it is a big deal. That volcano could blow at any time.

Brett: It could also do absolutely nothing for the next 10,000 years. I read all about volcanos in Earth Science, and I even did a project on one.

Maddie: Congratulations, Einstein. So you know what will happen when it explodes?

Brett: IF it explodes.

Maddie: WHEN it explodes we are going to be covered with ash and molten lava and be killed instantly.

Brett: We can get out in plenty of time.

Natalie: You think that the volcano is going to send us a text message that it's getting ready to blow half the mountain up into the air?

Maddie: Maybe an email?

They both were laughing at me. I hated them.

Maddie: If we can't find the bead we are going to have to find a new place to live. Somewhere far, far away from the volcano. We probably should do that anyway, just to be safe.

Brett: I'm not leaving my valley.

Natalie: Your valley?

Maddie: Come outside, Brett. Let me show you something else.

Brett: It's dark. You can't see anything. Der.

Maddie: I know. That's what I want to show you.

We all went outside. With no light pollution the stars always looked like that Vincent Van Gogh painting. Bigger than life. Awesome.

Maddie: Now look up.

Brett: I am looking up, doofus.

Natalie: Wow, look at that shooting star.

Maddie: That's not a shooting star. Or an airplane. Or a spaceship.

Brett: It could be a spaceship. Maybe they are coming back to get Natalie.

Natalie: You're a spaceship.

Brett: No, YOU'RE a spaceship.

Maddie: Shut up, dorkamatics. It's an asteroid or a meteor.

Natalie: How do you know?

Maddie: Because I've been watching it for the past few weeks while you guys were sleeping. It just keeps getting bigger and bigger. And closer and closer.

Brett: Chicxulub.

Natalie: Chick-fil-A?!? I love Chick-fil-A!

Brett: Chicxulub is the name of the impact crater near Mexico. Geophysicists discovered it in 1978.

Maddie: Brett, you're a regular miniature genius. How do you know all this weird stuff?

Brett: When I'm not playing video games, I read a lot.

Natalie: So, wait a minute. Like the big Meteor Crater we saw in Arizona that time? The one that left a gigantic hole in the ground?

Brett: Yeah, only about a billion times bigger. Like a million atomic bombs going off at once. A lot of paleontologists think that the impact at Chicxulub caused the extinction of the dinosaurs.

Natalie: O. M. G. That's what is coming right at us?!?!? I think I'd much rather have a blueberry muffin.

Brett: We don't know that. It's just a theory anyway.

Maddie: Who cares about the theory? If that thing hits Earth we are going to be blown to smithereens. Or at best die some long painful death from starvation or dehydration or strangulation.

Natalie: None of those things sound like much fun at all.

Brett: Maddie, you are just guessing. Whatever that thing is, it could miss us by 100,000 miles.

Maddie: Or it could land right on top of us.

Brett: Or not.

Maddie, grabbed me by one of my ears and started twisting.

Brett: Ouch...stop it!

Maddie: BRETT, THIS WORLD IS GOING TO END. YOU KNOW THAT. WE HAVE TO FIND A WAY TO GET OUT OF HERE. YOU NEED TO HELP US. NOW!!!

Brett: Ok, ok. No need to go bat-crap crazy. Let me think about it.

Natalie: I'm hungry.

After they went back inside, I watched the large object moving slowly across the sky. It was awesome and not awesome all at the same time. Boogers. Wet, slimy, sticky, giant boogers.

LAST DAY / THE FOURTH DIMENSION

What they didn't know and what I was never going to tell them is that I already knew exactly where the bead was. I had found it inside Dad's adventure hat one day when I was just sitting around doing nothing. There it was tucked underneath the disgusting sweatband on the inside of Dad's hat. I found it before Natalie and Maddie arrived, so I had no idea what it was. For some reason I just left it there and forgot it. When they started jabbering all about it, I remembered exactly where it was. I almost never wore the hat anymore, so it was safe and sound, hidden behind some rocks in the cave.

I had two big problems with the bead. First, I really didn't have any interest at all in going back to the modern world. My life was here now, and I loved it. Sure it was a little dangerous and unpredictable from time to time, but when I thought hard it about it those were the parts I liked the most. I was living my dreams. I wasn't just another out-of-shape fifth grader, sitting around bored to tears playing stupid video games (Did I really say that?). I was the hero of my own adventure. My life was awesome. Really awesome.

My other problem was that there was only one bead. One bead, three people. The math didn't work. Since none of us understood how the markers or the beads actually worked, that was a huge problem. Would one bead get all three of us back to Florida? Or would it get Maddie and Natalie home even if I could persuade them to go back without me? I knew Maddie was just trying to trick me into finding the beads and that she would force me to go back with them. Or at least she would try.

I half-heartedly helped them "look" for the beads, but I think they knew my heart wasn't in it. The rumblings from the volcano would go away for a couple of days, and then they would come back longer and stronger. One morning we awoke to the sound of thunderous roaring in the valley. It was way louder than any dinosaur could have been. We all rushed out of the cave and saw the last of the avalanche coming down the steep granite walls about half way down the valley. Maddie grabbed me by the shoulders.

Maddie: See that, Brett?!?!

Brett: Yes, please let go of me.

Natalie: Wow, that could have been us.

Maddie: Exactly. The volcano is shaking this whole valley to pieces. We HAVE to get out of here.

Natalie: Like yesterday.

Brett: So, we're just going to pack up and go...where?

Maddie: Somewhere a long, long way from here. This valley is just not safe. We could fly the Pterandons and do some scouting. Maybe we should move closer to the ocean.

Natalie: Ok gang, let's split up and look for clues.

Brett: Take it easy, Freddo, we are not going anywhere.

Maddie: Brett, it's not safe. We CAN NOT stay here. Since I'm the oldest, I'm making an executive decision. We are going to scout today, and tomorrow we are moving. End of story.

I knew that look on Maddie's face. I had seen it a million times. It wasn't any use arguing with her. I also had to admit she was right. That avalanche was only about a half a mile away. The next one might bury the cave and the waterfall in a trillion tons of boulders and debris. We would have no warning and no chance if it came roaring down the mountain. Stupid volcano.

We spent all that day flying around and looking for a new spot to call home. We had to fly all the way around the volcano to get to the ocean, because the ash and smoke were so thick we could barely see. There wasn't any place near the ocean that looked that great. Even though we had the ocean to protect us on one side, we were exposed on the other three. Was it even far enough from the volcano? I remembered my days in the tree house and how that had ended so badly. We would probably just have to keep moving up and down the coast until we found something suitable. Would the Pteranodons follow us there? I knew they loved to fish, but there weren't really any cliffs suitable for nesting. This whole thing was a complicated mess.

We didn't get back to the cave until it was almost dark. Everyone was exhausted after riding the pterosaurs all day. I was very depressed. Of course, the volcano was still rumbling like crazy.

Natalie: Brett, you should eat something. Try this soup. It's actually pretty yummy. Oviraptor.

Brett: Not hungry.

Maddie: You'll feel better after you eat something. I know you are upset about leaving, but we just don't have any other choice.

Brett: Still not hungry.

Maddie: Well, you are just going to have to accept this. It's not going to do any of us any good for you to sit around and pout like a baby. We need you to be fully engaged if we are going to survive.

Brett: Thanks for the lecture.

Natalie: It's going to be ok, Little Buddy. We'll find another place to live, and it will be even better than this one.

Brett: Until the meteor hits.

Maddie: I thought you said it was going to miss us.

Brett: Have you seen it lately? It's not moving across the sky anymore, but it just keeps getting bigger and bigger.

There wasn't much else to say. Everything got quiet, and we settled down for our last night in the cave. I slowly packed up everything I could in the Camelback, and put as much food as I could into the knapsack. I wasn't looking forward to starting over from scratch again. Oh well, like Dad always says: all good things gotta come to an end.

After the girls fell asleep, I finally crawled into my hammock. I thought about all the great times I experienced in this wonderful valley. Finding the waterfalls and the cave, learning how to survive, hunting for dinosaurs and teaching Skinny how to fly. This place was full of incredible memories. It made me so sad to think this part of my adventure was coming to an end.

I tossed and turned, and couldn't get any sleep. After a couple of hours, I finally rolled out of my hammock and crept outside for one last night of star-gazing in my beautiful valley. OH, WOW! The meteor was bigger than I had ever seen it. Was it on fire? Was it burning though the atmosphere? My heart was in my throat. I needed to find Dad's hat and the bead just in case we had to make an emergency escape.

As I stood up and turned around to go back into the cave, the sky burst above me. I just stood there dumbfounded as the volcano exploded the mountain into a million tiny pieces of rock, ash and flying lava. The ground was shaking so hard I had to reach out and grab a rock on the side of the cave just to hang on. Was I watching the greatest fireworks show in the history of the world?

The fire from the volcano lit up the night sky like a celestial stadium, and I watched with shock and awe as the earthquake split the valley below. The sky rained fire and ash and the smell of burning sulfur burned my throat. HOLY FREAKING APOCALYPSE!!!!

My mind started spinning a million miles an hour. The hat. The cave. MY SISTERS!

The earth stopped shaking for just a second, but my brain reminded me the aftershocks could be just as bad or worse. The falling ash and the steam from the now scalding waterfall were so thick, I could barely see. I desperately crawled through the burning rubble trying to find the entrance of the cave. It was blocked.

"MADDIE!"

"NATALIE!"

The burning rocks were scorching my hands as I desperately started digging through the rubble.

"MADDIE!"

"NATALIE!"

I thought I heard a muffled cry. Were they alive?!?! I finally made an opening and yelled through it.

"MADDIE! NATALIE! CAN YOU HEAR ME! ARE YOU GUYS OK?!?!"

I almost couldn't hear anything over the roar of the still exploding volcano, but finally there was a faint sound. Coughing.

"Brett, Brett. We're ok, but we are trapped."

"FIND THE HAT AND DIG YOUR WAY OUT. FOLLOW THE SOUND OF MY VOICE. OVER HERE!"

"The cat?!?!"

Seriously? "NO YOU DINGLEBERRIES...THE HAAAATTTTTTTTT!"

I was digging furiously, but the rocks were still landing all around me.

"HURRY!"

It seemed like forever, but finally, I saw a hand.

"DIG...DIG...DIG!!!"

We finally made a hole big enough to drag them both out one at a time. They were beaten and a little bloody, but otherwise in good shape. They just stood there watching our world getting blown to bits. Now in addition to the fire and rocks and molten lava, it was raining. Oh, wow. Lightning danced across the sky illuminating this cataclysmic destruction. It was hard not to be amazed. I noticed we were all holding hands.

"DID YOU BRING THE HAT?!?"

"THE BAT?"

"NO, DAD'S ADVENTURE HAT!!!"

"NATALIE HAS IT...IT'S RIGHT HERE."

I snatched it from Nat and quickly turned it inside out fumbling for the sweat band. WHERE WAS THAT STUPID BEAD?!?! I finally found it and when I showed it to them through the smoke and rain and steam and ash, I saw them grinning like monkeys.

"YOU SNEAKY, BRETT!!!"

"YOU GUYS READY TO GET THE HECK OUT OF HERE?!?!"

Just then Natalie screamed and pointed. We all looked up and saw the fiery meteor burst through the atmosphere and light up the sky like an exploding sun. I figured we had about a minute before we were burnt to a crisp.

Just then a gust of wind blew the hat and the bead out of my hand up, up, up into the air. What can go wrong, will go wrong. I cursed this evil night and the stupid markers that had brought us to this horrible end. My scream rose above the roar of the tumult surrounding us.

I don't know how Skinny heard that pitiful scream and/or how he had survived all the awfulness of the volcano, but there he was right at my side. Without thinking I leapt on his back and pulled my sisters on behind me. We took off in search of the hat, and the life-saving bead I hoped was still in it.

The falling, white-hot meteor scorched our faces, and flew downward through the night sky. Time was running out. The meteor would crash in seconds. I somehow miraculously spotted Dad's hat, spinning, flipping and dancing through the rain and smoke and ash.

"HANG ON...!!!!!"

I kicked Skinny into a barrel roll and we followed the elusive, twisting, turning hat. I have no idea how my sisters held on, but they must have because I saw Maddie reach out and snatch the hat out of mid-air.

"GOT IT!!!"

I reached back and she stuffed it into my hand. I looked into the rain-soaked, ash covered hat. NO BEAD!!! Wait, there it was! Somehow, someway, through everything the crazy bead was still sitting inside the hat. It must have blown back in. A miracle. AWESOME!!!

The meteor was breaking apart and flaming parts of it were whizzing by us and crashing into the ground, creating ear-splitting explosions and blinding light. It was all I could do to hold on. I leaned into Skinny's ear and shouted.

"WELL DONE, FELLA...YOU ARE THE BEST!

I tore off a piece of the bead and held it in my teeth. I handed Maddie the rest and I hoped she did the same thing. I glanced back and saw her pass the last, little piece to Natalie. The last thing I saw was the massive flaming meteor crash into my beloved valley. The deafening explosion blew all of us completely off Skinny. Farewell, friend. I saw Natalie reaching out for me. I grabbed her hand and then Maddie's. I swallowed. Everything went white and silent. I was spinning, spinning, spinning...

When I finally came to, it took me a few minutes to orient myself. I gradually realized I wasn't anywhere near the Colorado River.

But I WAS staring into the snarling face of a saber-toothed tiger. There was no sign of my sisters anywhere. Oh, wow. I passed out again.